Worship

Breaking Through to His Presence and Power

by

Norvel Hayes

D0104813

Unless otherwise indicated, all Scripture quotations are taken from the *King James Version* of the Bible.

Worship — Breaking Through to His Presence and Power
ISBN 978-1606830031
Copyright © 1993 by Norvel Hayes
P. O. Box 1379
Cleveland, Tennessee 37311

Contents

Introduction

God wants you to have victory in your life. He wants to give you everything you need or ever will need. He wants to give you the desires of your heart.

When you are willing to spend time in His presence, worshipping and praising Him, you will be amazed at what happens. His blessings will fall on you — totally fall on you.

There was a time that I didn't know worship and praise were important. I just thought that as long as I loved God and was faithful to Him, as long as I went to church, paid my tithes and was nice to people, things would turn out okay for me. But after I went into the ministry, I found out what really was involved in serving the Lord.

When I learned the things about worship and praise that I am going to share with you in this book, my life was changed. I found out that when I obeyed God's Word, it came alive to me and God was able to manifest Himself to me. I found out that He had already set up a covenant with His people and that He had provided its blessings just for me and for you.

Yes, there is a time to sing. There is a time to pray. There is a time to preach. There is a time to teach. There is a time to give thanks. There is a time to praise. But there is also a time to worship, and as you do and as I do we will begin to walk in all that God has provided for us and live day by day in a brand new realm.

1
"Worship Me More..."

1
"Worship Me More..."

Praise ye the Lord. I will praise the Lord with my whole
heart, in the assembly of the upright,
and in the congregation.

Psalm 111:1

Several years ago I was driving down the road just
minding my own business when the Spirit of God came
upon me. He comes upon me in some of the most
unusual places! Then He said to me, "Son, the church is
sadly lacking."

I said, "What do you mean, 'sadly lacking'?"

"Well," He said, "My children basically love Me, but
they live in poverty and sickness and defeat. They don't
live in heaven's blessings because they don't worship
Me enough."

"You said that right, Lord," I said. "In fact I know
whole congregations who don't spend any time
worshipping You at all. The pastors don't ever say,
'Let's worship God for a while just because He's God.'
They just teach the people to go to church, sing a few
songs and listen to a song or two sung by the choir, but
they don't really worship You."

Then He said to me, "And neither do you."

All I could say was, "Is that right?"

He continued, "You're going around the country teaching My Word. You're teaching faith and confession. You're praying for the sick, but you need to worship Me more, and you need to teach My people to worship Me more. I'm their God, and they're My children. If you'll teach my children to worship Me more, I'll do great and mighty things for them."

By this time I was weeping. Every time the Lord tells me I'm a flake and I've missed it, I always repent and weep. It wasn't long before I found out what the Bible said about worship and began to teach on worship.

God Wants You
To Live an Abundant Life

Do you know that I found out that God wanted to bless me? He wanted to give me peace and contentment. He wanted to give me strength without sorrow. Do you know that He wants to do the same for you?

That sick, poverty stricken, weak, confused, goofed up life some believers are living is not the kind of life He prepared for us. The kind of life He prepared for us is an abundant life.

You might be saying, "But, Brother Norvel, my children are backslidden. My husband is sick, and the doctors say that there is no hope for him. I've been asking myself, 'Why do all these things happen to me? Why doesn't God ever do something for me?'"

How much have you been worshipping God this month?

You might say, "I haven't worshipped Him any this month, but I go to a good church, and my pastor is nice."

Well, I don't doubt that you go to a good church and have a nice pastor, but what does that have to do with you? Your pastor and your church can't worship God for you. You're supposed to have a relationship with God yourself.

You might say, "But, Brother Norvel, I've been saved and baptized in the Holy Ghost for thirty years. God knows I love Him."

You didn't answer my question. Have you worshipped Jesus any this month? Have you bowed down before Him this month and called Him your Savior, your Healer and your Miracle Worker? Have you thanked Him because your name is written in heaven? Have you told Him how wonderful He is and worshipped Him and Him only?

"Well, as a matter of fact, I don't think I have."

Then you're missing the abundant blessings from heaven! Worship is important to God!

God finds so much favor in His children when He looks down and sees them worshipping and praising Him. He's working out their problems for them. He gives them everything they need and want that's in the Bible. He brings to pass the desires of their hearts. (Ps. 37:4.)

It doesn't matter what kind of problems you have. God knows what to do. I don't know what to do, but Jesus does. He knows all about your case. He made you.

He loves you and wants to bless you. All He wants you to do is worship Him for Who He is and praise Him for what He has done. Worship and praise are like twins; they just kind of mingle together.

"Get Alone Before Me"

When God showed me what I had been doing, I said, "Well, I don't know about the church, Jesus, but I'm going to change." I didn't change overnight, but over a period of time I began to go in the back room alone, bow myself down and just worship God myself.

I was traveling all over the country speaking to thousands of people. But until that day came, I really didn't spend any time worshipping God in my back room by myself. Oh, I prayed before a service to try to get an anointing from Him, and I tried to live my life right. But I didn't spend any quality time by myself in my room alone, where no man sees.

If you have to have a bunch of people around you before you can worship God, your relationship with God is half sick. You shouldn't have to have anybody with you to worship God. Your worship to God never will please Him to the fullest until He sees you do it alone.

If you want God to bless you out of your socks, start worshipping Him in your bedroom by yourself. Sure, God is pleased when you worship Him in church, but those choruses you sing before a service are to train you to worship. They're not going to get the job done. God is pleased with it, but you're going to have to come to a place that you decide you're going to have a relationship with God yourself, just you and Him.

You can't live on your mother's relationship with Him. You can't live on your daddy's relationship with Him. You can't live on your pastor's relationship with Him. You have to have a relationship with God yourself, and you'll never have a relationship that is worth much to you unless you learn to put first things first. **Seek ye first the kingdom of God, and his righteousness; and all these things shall be added unto you** (Matt. 6:33).

When you put first things first, it won't be very long until God will begin to visit you in a new way. Your mouth will taste like it has sugar in it. The atmosphere around you will smell like roses because Jesus is the Rose of Sharon. (Song 2:1.)

If I could just talk you into believing the Scripture in Matthew 6:6 that says if God sees you pray in secret He will reward you openly, you would see the reality of this Scripture for yourself. If people reading this book would actually begin worshipping Him by themselves, I would be getting letters from some of them next year and the next year and the next year saying, "Brother Norvel, I worshipped God for a year and a few little things happened, but now my life has begun to change totally. Life isn't a struggle for me anymore. God is showering me with His blessings. I can hardly stand it."

Since That Day

Now are you ready for this? Since the day I started doing this, I've had no financial problems. I even bought some property for a Bible school. In a year the ministry had the money to pay for it. We never even had to take up an offering!

"You mean to tell me you never had to take up an offering to pay for the building?"

Honey, I mean to tell you that we've got four sanctuaries now — we're putting the finishing touches on the fourth one now — and I never took up an offering to pay for one of them.

You say, "Well, where did the money come from?"

I don't know. It just showed up. God would send to a seminar where I was speaking people who would say, "Brother Norvel, I was praying in the state where I'm from, and God told me to come here and give you a check for ten thousand dollars."

Now I haven't lived my life a hundred percent perfect. There's only been one Jesus, and I'm not Him. There's only been One Who didn't make any mistakes, and I'm not Him. But if you'll just try to do what He tells you to do, the blessings of God will fall on you, totally fall on you.

One year I was in Columbus, Ohio, to speak at a camp meeting. When I arrived at the motel that day, I told the pastor I wouldn't be meeting with him that afternoon but that I would see him that night.

All afternoon I stayed in my room and worshipped God. I must have worshipped Him for about five or six hours. That evening when I spoke at camp meeting, I opened up my mouth, and God began revealing and unfolding the Bible to me. I could have taught the Bible for ten hours and never looked at it. It was just coming to me in revelation knowledge like you would not believe. I mean it was just absolutely pouring out from me.

And the anointing — I could hardly stand it. I thought God was going to take me to heaven. I got so anointed that at first I could hardly talk! Another minister who was sitting next to the pastor said: "Norvel is anointed so heavy. I don't see how he's standing up. He may just fall on the floor any minute." During that meeting the Holy Spirit moved in such a powerful way. It's amazing what He will do when you obey His Word and worship Him.

Make Worship and Praise a Way of Living

You may want to choose a particular time and place for worship. That's fine if you do. It's up to you. I don't do that, but you can if that's how you feel.

If you set a time — say, 6:00 or 9:00 in the morning, for instance — to worship God, don't say later: "Well, I worshipped God for an hour this morning, so my time has already been spent in worship. I can do something else now." No, you need to be ready and willing to worship God anytime.

I am not telling you that you have to get up at 5:00 in the morning and keep worshipping God until 9:00. And you don't have to go out under an oak tree at 3:00 every afternoon so that you can praise God for three hours.

I've tried all those kinds of things, and it all sounds really religious and really good, but the sad part of it is you can never stick to it. There will come a day when you can't go out under the oak tree at 3:00 and pray for three hours. Do you understand that?

It is a good idea to establish a time and place for worship and praise if you want to. I am not knocking that. But don't let a schedule and place for prayer put you under some kind of pressure or bondage. Just make worship and praise a way of living.

I worship God regularly, but I don't have hours set to worship Him. I try to worship Him at least two, three or four times a day. Personally, when I first get up every morning, I like to worship the Lord for a while.

"For how long, Brother Norvel?" people ask me.

I don't know how long. I'm not going to time myself in worshipping God. I got delivered from that bondage a long time ago! I used to worship God only from 11:00 to 12:00 every Sunday morning. But if we didn't get out at 12:00, the other churches would beat us to the cafeteria!

God doesn't wear a watch. He has nothing but time. If you want to worship God every morning, take five, ten, fifteen minutes — take three hours if you want to.

But watch that you don't get out too far and get weird. If you do, it won't be long till you'll want to quit your job and "live by faith." After three or four months, your wife will be saying, "Have you looked at the cupboards lately?" You'll say, "I'm just believing God to supply our needs, honey." After about six months of that she'll be saying, "Don't you 'honey' me. I'm hungry."

Make worshipping God a way of living, but stay balanced I'm telling you. God likes *normal* people full of the Holy Ghost.

Maybe you're a businessman, and you want to worship God at noontime in your office. Well then, just close the door to your office and say to your secretary, "If I get any phone calls, take a message. Get the number, and I'll return the call."

Just show God that you'll close your office door for fifteen minutes. Then don't do anything while you're alone there in your office except worship and praise Him. Get down on your knees and praise Him and worship Him for a while. Start seeing Jesus as your business partner. After spending some time like that, the glory of the Lord will start coming into your office and you'll begin to feel His presence like never before.

When you begin to worship God alone, He will reward you openly. In God there is no defeat. Whenever you suffer an unsuccessful thing in your life, it is because Jesus is on the outside looking in. He is not involved in it. Anything that Jesus gets involved in will be successful. There are no unsuccessful things in God. Everything in God is successful.

Praise Him in the Congregation

Now just because you worship God alone doesn't mean you shouldn't ever worship Him when others are around. Psalm 111:1 says, **Praise ye the Lord. I will praise the Lord with my whole heart, in the assembly of the upright, and in the congregation.** God said to praise Him with the upright and in the congregation

When I was in Tulsa, Oklahoma, one time, I found out quickly about what happens when people praise and worship in the congregation. While I was staying with Brother Kenneth Hagin and his wife, Oretha, we went out to a restaurant for dinner one night.

We had left the table and were walking across the dining room when, all of a sudden, a man stopped me at his table and said, "Norvel Hayes?"

"Yes, sir," I said.

"I won't take much of your time. I know you are with Brother and Sister Hagin. But sometimes people don't ever give you testimonies. I just want to give you a quick one."

"I was a total dope addict," he said. "I had been on dope about sixteen years. I was a needle case, a heavy trip. One night I was strung out on drugs and, as I was driving by a big building, I saw hundreds of cars in the parking lot. I was so strung out that I didn't know what was going on.

"I thought to myself, 'They must be having a big party in there. Look at all the cars!' So I parked my car.

"Somehow I found my way to the building and went inside. You were up there behind the pulpit speaking, so I took a seat toward the back of the room.

"Then you had people stand up. I was just standing there, totally strung out on drugs. I didn't even know where I was. I didn't know what was going on. I had never heard of Kenneth Hagin.

"You pointed your finger straight at me and said, 'Lift up your hands and praise God. He is worthy to be praised.'

"When you said that, I just thought, 'Well, I'll just lift up my hands and praise God.'

"All of a sudden some kind of power came right down from the top of my head. It went through my hands and out the bottom of my feet. When it did, every bad desire left me. I sobered up and became normal right at that moment.

"I was totally changed into another human being as I stood there that night, because you told me to lift up my hands and praise God. You said that God would do great things for me, that the works of God were great. When I lifted up my hands, every ounce of bad desire left me completely.

"Today I am a student at Brother Hagin's school, Rhema Bible Training Center, and I just wanted to thank you, Mr. Hayes, for your ministry."

If you want God to help you and bless you abundantly, learn to worship Him and praise Him. If it will work for a dope addict, it will work for you, but you can't be ashamed of God in front of men. Praise Him with your own mouth out loud so you can hear yourself praising Him, and worship Him with your whole heart in the assembly of the upright and in the congregation.

Your Motive Is Important

Now some people try to be religious with God on Sunday morning and Sunday night then do their own thing the rest of the week. Why don't they worship God all through the week?

Some people take you out to dinner and want to show you how religious they are and say, "Bless God, I've got some tracts with me, and I'm going to get this waitress saved." Then they say to the waitress, "Hey, are you saved?"

Do you know why those people are like that? Basically it is because they want to be seen in public. They don't spend any quality time worshipping Jesus in the back room where nobody can see them. God plainly tells us in His Word that they already have their reward. **Take heed that ye do not your alms before men, to be seen of them: otherwise ye have no reward of your Father which is in heaven** (Matt. 6:1).

When you act like this, you're not helping Jesus. Do you understand that? You don't have to show somebody how spiritual you are by embarrassing somebody else or by stopping somebody on their job while someone is paying them to be working.

If the situation calls for it and you feel led of the Lord, that's fine, but always remember not to get out of order. Learn how to conduct yourself first of all. Always leave a person with a good taste in his mouth about you and Jesus.

We have all made mistakes in our lives. Sometimes when people get baptized in the Holy Spirit, they run around the country trying to share messages in tongues with everybody. Now God would like for everybody to speak in tongues, I guarantee you, but people shouldn't run around doing that.

They think, "Now that I am baptized in the Holy Ghost and I speak with other tongues, I am going to go home and get my whole family baptized in the Holy Ghost and speaking with other tongues!" No. They need to take a different approach.

If they go home and say that to their families, the whole bunch may say, "*What*? You do *what*?"

I know a beautiful girl who was baptized in the Holy Ghost and spoke with other tongues. Then she went home and told her husband, "I speak in other tongues!" He got so scared of her that he wouldn't kiss her again. He said, "You're not kissing me! You have one of those funny spirits."

They wound up getting a divorce.

Somebody (probably other than his wife) should have taken the Bible and sat down with him, shown him the Scriptures (1 Cor. 14; Acts 2:4), and explained to him intelligently about the plan of salvation and the baptism in the Holy Spirit with the evidence of speaking in other tongues. Handling it that way would have given him a chance to understand it. At least, he might have understood it a little bit.

But she just blazed away at him with: "I've got what you need. You need to be baptized in the Holy Ghost and speak with other tongues."

She told the truth, but she didn't handle it right. So she got no more kisses, and it wasn't long until she was divorced.

Watch what you say and how you act around people. Be led by God in everything you do. Then you will always conduct yourself the way He wants you to.

2
The Works of the Lord Are Great!

2

The Works of the Lord Are Great!

**The works of the Lord are great, sought out of all them
that have pleasure therein.**

Psalm 111:2

"What exactly do the works of the Lord include,
Brother Norvel?" you may ask.

The works of the Lord are salvation for you and
your whole family if your faith waivereth not. The
works of the Lord God Almighty are health to your
body. The works of the Lord are miracles when you
need them. The works of the Lord are the nine gifts of
the Spirit for anyone that will believe in Him. **The
works of the Lord are great, sought out of all them that
will have pleasure therein** (v. 2).

I wish the world knew how great the works of the
Lord were. I hate to have to say this, but I wish all the
church world knew it, too. I know that some of them do,
but I feel so sorry for the people who are always working
hard to build buildings in their own strength instead of
enjoying the great works of the Lord. They are sweet
people who spend lots of money, millions of dollars, on
buildings for the Lord. But because of the doctrine they
are living under, the doctrine that is preached to them,
they may never get to enjoy the works of God.

19

"But, Brother Norvel, I'm sick. I'm broke. I'm confused. I need help."

I'm telling you boldly that the works of God are great, and they are manifested when you are willing to worship and praise Him.

As long as you reject worshipping God and praising Him and glorifying His name, you will have no knowledge of His works' being great. You will be leaving Jesus out of your life because you are failing to keep your eyes on Him.

The Works of the Lord Are Healing

Some Jews in Jerusalem saw some of the healing works of the Lord, and they were amazed at what they saw. Let's read about this in Acts 3.

> Now Peter and John went up together into the temple at the hour of prayer, being the ninth hour.
>
> And a certain man lame from his mother's womb was carried, whom they laid daily at the gate of the temple which is called Beautiful, to ask alms of them that entered into the temple;
>
> Who seeing Peter and John about to go into the temple asked an alms.
>
> And Peter, fastening his eyes upon him with John, said, Look on us.
>
> And he gave heed unto them, expecting to receive something of them.
>
> Then Peter said, Silver and gold have I none; but such as I have give I thee: In the name of Jesus Christ of Nazareth rise up and walk.
>
> And he took him by the right hand, and lifted him up: and immediately his feet and ankle bones received strength.

And he leaping up stood, and walked, and entered with them into the temple, walking, and leaping, and praising God.

And all the people saw him walking and praising God:

And they knew that it was he which sat for alms at the Beautiful gate of the temple: and they were filled with wonder and amazement at that which had happened unto him.

verses 1-10

Within a few minutes that crippled man was totally normal. His leg wasn't crooked anymore! And he went walking, and leaping, and praising God! When the Jews saw it, they were amazed.

"But Jews don't believe in Jesus, Brother Norvel," someone may say.

When they see a crippled man healed, they do all of a sudden. You would, too, especially if you had someone who was crippled at home yourself. You would believe it quickly!

Oh, I have pleasure in the works of the Lord. And, my friend, you should have pleasure in them, too.

The Works of the Lord Are Financial Provision

As I shared before, God said to me: "I want My people to spend time worshipping Me. I want to see My church worship. But more than that I want individuals to worship Me, especially when those individuals get alone before Me."

When God told me that, I began to worship Him more and more. I began to spend time worshipping and praising Him. When I put Him first in worship and praise, finances began to come to me and to my ministry.

The same thing will work within your church. But your pastor and the congregation have to want to worship God. They have to spend more time worshipping God and praising Him, looking toward heaven rather than always seeing the needs and the lack of money.

Put everything in the proper perspective. Then God will provide, and you will see hundreds of thousands of dollars added to your church's account. I'm telling you that you will.

You may say, "Well, where does it come from, Brother Norvel?"

Who in the world knows where it comes from? I don't always know myself. God will just see that it comes.

I received an interesting letter at my office one day. This is how it read:

> I'm down here in Florida and I was praying. Brother Norvel, the Lord told me to send your ministry a check for $26,000.
>
> I told my wife about it, but she didn't agree with me. I said, "Honey, I know what the Lord told me. I was praying and God told me to send Norvel Hayes's ministry a check for $26,000. So you go pray yourself and ask God about it."

She went to her room and started praying. After she had prayed for a while, she came out and said, "Send Brother Norvel the check."

And he did! My friend, that happens to me all the time. *All* the time!

My ministry has money in the bank, but we need it with all that's required at our office and in our Bible school. There is always something that needs to be done. I believe we ought to have a certain amount of money just as a nest egg. Then when something comes up, I don't have to say, "Where are we going to get the money?" I can tell you right now, God doesn't want me to worry about anything.

The Works of the Lord Are Gifts From the Spirit

One time when I was holding a meeting in San Antonio, Texas, a lady came up to be prayed for. When I laid my hands on her and prayed, she raised up her hands and began to praise the Lord. All of a sudden she broke down and began to weep.

It seemed different with her as she was praising the Lord. Both of her hands were being held out as if she were playing a piano. As she continued praising Jesus, her body was standing still, but both her hands were moving from left to right. She was praising the Lord with her mouth and with her hands, and tears were streaming down her face.

She must have stood there for about twenty minutes. When I looked around at her, the Spirit of God said to me, "I'm teaching her to play the organ."

As we saw in Psalm 111:2, the works of God are great. But you will never know much about the great works of God until you bow down before Him and begin to worship. To worship Him, you have to spend some time praising His name and glorifying Him.

This woman's husband was standing with her by this time. I walked over to them and said to her, "The Holy Ghost just spoke to me, and He is teaching you to play the organ."

After that happened, God unfolded the organ to her and taught her to play it by ministering to her through her hands. She began to play the organ just like a professional. She was so good, in fact, that the pastor of a large congregation in Houston, Texas, had her come to his church and play for them. She was so good at the organ that she played there for months and months.

The Works of the Lord Are for the Next Generation

If you will give your talent to God and dedicate yourself to Him, God will do the same kind of work in your offspring that He has done in you.

I saw this happen through a mother and daughter after I ministered another time in San Antonio, Texas. I met a lady who was a viola player in the San Antonio symphony orchestra.

She said, "Norvel, would you come to my house, talk to my husband, and beg him to let me work for Jesus?"

I had dinner with them and talked for a long time about the importance of their being open to the Lord's work.

"You're not married to a normal girl," I said to the husband. "Your wife has a deep dedication to God, and she is heavily anointed of God. He is going to do great and mighty things for her, because she would go anywhere for Him."

She was willing to drive five hundred miles to play one tune on the viola for Jesus. One time she drove to Shreveport, Louisiana, where I was holding a meeting. When she started to play the viola, the Lord healed a crippled man who was sitting down front. Then people started being healed everywhere.

All she did was play the viola as God led her.

When you start praising God with the stringed instruments and with your voice, it is amazing what God will do. He just wants His people to praise Him.

First, that lady used her stringed instrument to praise the Lord. Then she was blessed when a baby girl was born to her. When that daughter grew into her teens, the Lord God gave her a singing voice. He anointed that voice; and by the age of fifteen, she was given the ability to write songs.

Now that young lady is exactly like her mother. She will go anywhere, anyplace, whenever she is allowed to do something for Jesus.

The Works of the Lord Are Already Prepared for You

The works of the Lord are great, and they are available to all who would worship and praise God for all He has done and ever will do for us. When you worship and praise God, it's as if you are sitting down at God's table set with beautiful dishes and abundant food. Everything you will ever need in your life has been set before you on God's table. Every dish on His table has a big engraved sign with words like Salvation, Healing, Faith, Miracles, Deliverance, Knowledge, Wisdom.

The food inside is already prepared for you. You don't have to hire anybody to prepare it. It has already been prepared and paid for. All you have to do is get yourself in shape so that you can sit down and freely eat from God's table where His great works are available to you through His Word.

You get yourself in shape by building your faith and learning the promises of God to you in His Word. **So then faith cometh by hearing, and hearing by the word of God** (Rom. 10:17). You get yourself in shape by spending time in prayer. But you also get yourself in shape by praising and worshipping God, and letting it become a part of your life. Worship and praise God all the time you can. Then when you want something from God, you will come to His table and sit down with great manners, with great respect for His Word and His promises in it. You will put your napkin across your lap and sit up straight. Then you will look over and say, "Pass the healing bowl, please."

When it is passed, you will take that healing bowl and you will freely dip out of it. You will freely eat out of the bowl of His Word. Of course, when you eat God's Word, no matter what the subject is, you will start enjoying it more and more.

The kind of lifestyle you have will be based on the food you eat. If you are sick and don't know how to be healed, or haven't been healed, it is because you haven't been eating God's healing verses in the New Testament.

"Brother Norvel, I read about them."

Don't just read them, eat them. Meditate on them and make them part of you!

"But, Brother Norvel, I need a miracle," you say.

Sit down at God's table by worshipping and praising Him. Show His Word respect and with good manners say, "Pass the miracle bowl, please. I've got a big spoon!"

Reach into that miracle bowl and take out the miracle you need. Eat as much of it as you can stand because miracles are yours! God has miracle-working power, and it is a free gift to the church.

The Lord said to me: "Son, the reason many people can't receive is that they can't even eat at My table without being a nervous wreck. They haven't built up their faith. Their prayer life is shabby. They have hardly spent any time praising and worshipping Me."

The table is already set and prepared by Christ Jesus for you to live the abundant life (John 10:10), so eat anything you want from God's Word that you need. It is all in there.

"When they come to My table to eat," God told me, "the only reason they don't receive is that they have sloppy manners." When they are half-beaten, they sit down at the table and look over at the bowl of healing, hoping to get healed, but wondering, "Will it work for me?"

If your mind thinks like that, you won't receive the miracle you need! Renew your mind to the Word of God. You have the mind of Christ in you! When you do, you will sit down at God's table with respect and say: "Praise God! The stripes on Jesus' back have paid for my healing. So pass me that bowl of healing!" Then you will take it, fill your plate full of it, and eat it. As you eat it, you will chew every bite of it. You will gladly take in every mouthful, and you will receive it with dignity.

You won't be sloppy and let it run down your cheeks, because you don't want to miss even one drop of it. You don't want it to get away. You want every ounce of it and every bite of it. That is called having respect for the stripes on Jesus' back. It is called having respect for the healing verses in the Bible. Don't you know that the only part of the Bible you get to enjoy is the part you have respect for? And if you don't enjoy the Bible as much as a Hershey bar or homemade fudge with nuts, then go worship God some more.

As you worship God and praise Him, not only will you begin to desire to know what God's Word says, but it will become more appetizing to you, and you will be able to experience more and more of the abundant life that He has prepared for you.

The works of the Lord are great. Seek after them and have pleasure in them. (Ps. 111:2.)

3
Worship God,
and He Will Pay the Bills!

3

Worship God,
and He Will Pay the Bills!

He hath given meat unto them that fear him. . . .
Psalm 111:5

I want us to look at Psalm 111 again. This time at verses 3-5:

His work is honourable and glorious: and his righteousness endureth for ever.

He hath made his wonderful works to be remembered: the Lord is gracious and full of compassion.

He hath given meat unto them that fear him....

Don't Worship False Gods

If people aren't afraid to worship a false god, they can just go ahead and do it. But when they do, they may have to go without meat. Whole countries may starve because they don't worship God. They just don't worship God.

If those people would bow down before God and begin to worship Him with no shame, I guarantee you that it wouldn't be many days until the rain would start to fall and their crops would begin to grow.

If they kept on worshipping God, it wouldn't be long until they would have so much food that they

31

could sell it to other nations. They would be overloaded with food.

Just remember this: God will only put up with people's rejection of Him and their refusing to worship Him and glorify His name for just so long. God is full of mercy and compassion and understanding. (Ps. 86:15; 147:5.) Sometimes He will put up with what people do for years and years and years, even hundreds of years. But a nation can't continue rejecting the Lord Jesus Christ or failing to glorify Him and praise Him after He has shed His blood by suffering on the cross for all mankind without the devil wreaking havoc in the lives of its people. People like that don't even recognize God. They recognize some goofy false god.

Can you believe that any part of the human race could ever worship a false god, like Buddha for instance?

If I were going to worship any other god besides Jesus, I think I could find somebody that looked a little better than Buddha. I mean, if you are going to be deceived, you might as well be deceived in a nicer way. How people can ever worship him is beyond my understanding. I guess they do it because their parents taught them to. Everything produces after its own kind.

Experience His Abundant Life

Are you healthy? Are your needs met? Are you willing to do what God says, even if it means going out on the streets and passing out tracts? Does money mean anything to you?

If you have to say no to these questions, you are being robbed of living that precious abundant life in Jesus.

You may say, "Well, I don't believe Christians are supposed to have much money."

If you believe that, you are being robbed! Some people don't even know the truth that is in the Bible. They have no earthly idea about the things God would like for them to experience. They may have gone to church for years, but spiritually they are as empty as any person could possibly be.

They are good people who go to church and say, "I love the Lord...I love the Lord...I love the Lord." And they do love the Lord. But they have no earthly idea about living the precious life that Jesus has provided for them.

I know lots of people like this. And they are sweet people, too. I have gone over to their houses and had dinner with them. I love them all, every one of them. They are precious people.

But if I started talking to them about abundant life and said something like, "The Holy Ghost wants to make you a million dollars," they would almost come apart at the seams!

I want you to look at the next chapter, Psalm 112. You're not ready for it, but you might as well look at it anyway.

> **Praise ye the Lord. Blessed is the man that feareth the Lord, that delighteth greatly in his commandments.**
>
> **His seed shall be mighty upon earth: the generation of the upright shall be blessed.**
>
> **Wealth and riches shall be in his house: and his righteousness endureth for ever.**
>
> **verses 1-3**

Jesus wants you to live an abundant life! It's never God's will for you to be poor, to live in poverty, confusion and sickness. That is not God's will for the human race. I am telling you that if you will just bow down before God and worship Him and allow your mouth to praise and glorify His name, you'll get delivered.

You can live afar if you want to — far from where you could be living. You can wallow around in the lap of religion if you want to. Many people do, you know, even though they are good people who love the Lord.

But if those good people love the Lord, why don't they get God's best? They will never be able to get God's best until they bow down before God, worshipping Him and praising His name.

Let Your Soul Prosper First

When I began to spend time worshipping the Lord, finances began to come to me and to my ministry. I remember one time when the financial blessing came to me through a business deal. When I walked in that lawyer's office that morning to sign those papers, I said to Jesus, "I know when I sign those papers that I'll make a quarter of a million dollars. Now why did You do that for me? I don't even need it."

He said, "You passed My test."

I said, "Passed Your test? What do You mean that I passed Your test? I'm not any more special than anybody else."

He said, "You passed My test. Your soul has been prospering. You've been spending time worshipping Me, and you've been a witness for eight years to a woman who has been living in adultery. After eight years of compassion and eight years of love, that calls for rewards. Then He reminded me, "Who made a phone call to you so you could get this deal?"

I started thinking back, "Well, let me see now. Oh, that woman."

He said, "Yeah, and while she was living in adultery with that married man for eight years, you talked to her about heaven. You got her so hungry for heaven that she finally gave up her lover and got saved. That's the way it works. You let your soul prosper first."

God puts it this way in His Word, **Beloved, I wish above all things that thou mayest prosper and be in health, even as thy soul prospereth** (3 John 2). In another Scripture He says it another way: **But seek ye first the kingdom of God, and his righteousness; and all these things shall be added unto you** (Matt. 6:33). If you will seek Him first, God will add His abundant blessing to you.

You might say, "Brother Norvel, God is not adding abundant blessing to me."

Well, there is a reason why He is not. Now let me ask you a question, "Are you spending time every day worshipping God? Are you letting the praises of God come out of your mouth throughout the day?" When you do, God will release His power to you.

God Provides for the Needs of a Ministry

Some time ago I was at a convention where a well-known television evangelist was the speaker. During that time he shared with me about how his ministry had been having some problems.

"I'm having trouble paying my bills, Norvel. Since all this mess came out about the TV ministers, some stations haven't wanted to keep us on the air. I'm really having a problem."

At the end of the convention, they were holding a great big banquet. They called and said they wanted me to sit on the platform that day, so I did.

Then one of the fellows in charge came up to me and said, "Norvel, we're behind a lot."

"What do you mean?"

"Well, we've got to have several thousand dollars in this offering to even pay the bills for this convention. This is the last service. Why don't you pray and see if God will let you take up the offering for us?"

"Well, I'll pray, but I don't feel anything right now."

I know God calls me to do things like that sometimes, and I don't mind if the Spirit of God wants me to. So I prayed, but I didn't feel anything one way or the other.

A little while later, he came back over to me and said, "Norvel, do you feel like you can take up the offering for us?"

"Not necessarily," I said. "If you feel led of the Lord, you go ahead and take it up. If you don't feel like the Lord wants you to, then I'll take it up for you."

So it wasn't very long before he introduced me. The television evangelist was the banquet speaker, and he was sitting right next to me on the platform.

When I went up to the podium, I began to tell them about how I used to have to struggle sometimes to pay my bills until the Lord spoke to me about how I was missing it. Then I shared with them some of the things I have written in this book.

"The Lord said to me, 'You don't worship Me enough. You are going about the country establishing your own doctrines and doing your own thing.'"

Then I said to them: "So when you go around the country establishing your own doctrine, doing your own thing, preaching your own sermons, and praying your own prayers, God will let you pay your TV bills, too.

"He will let you take years and years and years to raise the money to build a building. He won't do anything about it. You will have to practically beg every church group that you come to, go on a money-raising campaign, and beat your members over the tops of their heads, trying to get them all to give money for this 'great campaign for God.'

"But the Lord told me that I could have anything I wanted in the Bible if I would worship Him. This convention needs several thousand dollars to pay the bills, but that is nothing for God."

Then I said: "Do you know what is going to happen? We are going to worship God in this place, and God is going to pay His bills. He will prove Himself to you."

About that time we started worshipping God. While we were worshipping, the Spirit of God all of a sudden came on me, and God began to boil a message out of my belly in tongues. I was weeping before God. When I spoke the message out in tongues, another man got up and gave the interpretation.

The evangelist began to weep and cry as he sat there. He wept and wept and wept, and so did a lot of other people.

I told the people to obey God in the offering. Because they had been worshipping God, they just freely gave into that offering. When the plates were passed, that offering came to much more than was needed. The convention bills were paid, and there was even some left over. That's no big deal for God!

When I had finished taking the offering, I patted that evangelist on the shoulder and said, "God bless you." He was still sobbing.

Then he was introduced. When he got to the podium, he said, "This coming Monday morning there is going to be a change at my ministry headquarters. Starting at 8:00 A.M. when all of my staff comes in, we are going to begin the day by worshipping God."

When he said that, I knew just how valuable that time of worship would be to them. When a group is willing to begin a time of worship and praise together like that, they can expect God to be in their midst — and their bills will be paid, too!

When you worship God during offering time, you can give what you want to. But when you really bow down in worship to God, you will *want* to give Him something. You don't need somebody to put pressure on you. Do you understand that?

Worship God, and you will want to give God something. It will be a privilege for you to give God something. It will be just like Jesus said: **...freely ye have received, freely give** (Matt. 10:8). You will freely give God something because you love Him and worship Him.

I have news for you: when you give God something freely, He will freely give it back to you. The only "trouble" you might have is that when He gives it back to you, He multiplies it many times. That is His way of blessing you like never before!

When that ministry staff did as the evangelist said they would and turned to worshipping God on a regular basis, they began to see victory like never before. And so will you...*if* you spend that same kind of time in worship and praise to your Lord Jesus Christ.

Worshipping God Brings You out of Debt

One of the most important things in the world that you can do is learn how to praise the Lord. Don't be afraid of praising Him. Be willing to learn how to praise your God.

Notice Psalm 112:1 says:

Praise ye the Lord. Blessed is the man that feareth the Lord, that delighteth greatly in his commandments.

I would be afraid not to praise God. After studying the Bible as much as I have, I know how important it is to God when we are willing to spend this kind of time before Him.

I have found that if I don't worship God and praise Him a curse can come on me.

"What do you mean a curse comes upon you, Brother Norvel?" someone may ask.

Well, a curse would be my not having enough money to pay the bills or having to put up with all kinds of problems. As believers, we do have afflictions (which the Lord delivers us from, according to Psalm 34:19), but I have noticed that when I don't spend time worshipping and praising the Lord, I end up having to put up with all kinds of problems all the time. There is no total freedom or victory.

A number of years ago when I was in Hawaii for another meeting, a fellow came up to me for counseling. He said: "I go to church here, Brother Norvel, and I really need some counseling. Could you help me?" Then he told me his situation.

"I have three children, and I haven't had a job in two years. I'm $15,000 in debt, and I've exhausted every angle for money.

"I've worked in the sugar cane fields here in Hawaii. But big corporations have come in and taken over. Little fellows like me can't get any more jobs. I have some big equipment just sitting out here, and I haven't turned a wheel on it in two years.

"I don't have any money for food, so I have to get food stamps and do what I can. My own children asked me for lunch money so they could eat with the other kids, but I had to tell them I don't have it. You know, that makes a daddy feel real bad when he has to say no to his own kids. But I can't give it to them when I don't have it.

"My friends have loaned me money, but I can't borrow any more. Can you help me, Brother Norvel?"

"Can I help you? I can tell you how to become rich!"

"Really?"

"Yes, really. But you have to listen to me. You have to listen and do what the Word of God says to do."

So I took Scripture and said, "Let's see what Jesus said." Then we looked at Mark 11:23, where Jesus said:

> ...Whosoever shall say unto this mountain, Be thou removed, and be thou cast into the sea; and shall not doubt in his heart, but shall believe that those things which he saith shall come to pass; he shall have whatsoever he saith.

Then I said to him: "Your whole world is framed with what you are saying. All the things you have said to me are: 'I don't do...,' 'I can't do...,' 'I'm broke,' 'I'm defeated.'"

"You are not talking right, and you will always be broke as long as you talk like that. You have to start daily changing your view on your life. You have to put your equipment together and get it ready to start working.

"I'm going to break the power of the Devil over you
and the power that is against you financially. We will
bind the Devil and run him off, in Jesus' name."

Then I told him how to command corporations to
call him and give him some big jobs that he could fill.

"I want you to begin to say, 'Now, big corporations,
I'm talking to you and I command you, in Jesus' name,
to call me and give me some jobs.' Now don't say 'job'
singularly; say 'jobs.' And don't say 'little jobs.' That's
foolish. Say 'big jobs.'"

"But, Norvel, they won't call me because they don't
call independents anymore."

"Hush your mouth! You're $15,000 in debt,
remember? Your equipment hasn't moved a wheel in
two years. Start seeing work coming your way, in Jesus'
name."

That is the truth. You may hate to have to tell people
the truth, because they are nice people, and the truth
can be so strong. But sometimes you have to. The only
thing I know is what I have learned from God. I am not
so smart myself, but I have learned to obey the Lord.

Then I said to him: "Now I want you to listen to me
and do what I tell you. I want us to get down on our
knees before God. I am going to teach you how to
worship Him. We are going to worship Jesus together
without shame.

"You need to start worshipping the Lord every
morning. Learn to praise Him with your mouth. Before
you start believing God to work in your behalf, you

have got to start thanking Him for all that He is. Spend time worshipping Him every day. Look to Him in worship and praise. Give Him thanks for all He has done for you."

"Well, Norvel," he said, "I do that sometimes. I do it in church."

"Well, you have to start talking to the Lord every day. Don't wait until you get to church to worship Him."

He listened to me and was willing to begin a change in his life when it came to putting His eyes on the Lord.

A few years later I saw him again.

"Norvel," he said, "I never forgot what you told me. Years ago you said that I would have to worship God every morning and praise Him in order for my circumstances to change."

"Yes, that's right. That's what I told you."

So after that he began to worship God without shame. He thanked God for all that God had done and all that God would do in his life. He and his wife even got together as a team to bow down before God and worship Him.

After they did that first, then he began to say, "Big corporations, you call me and give me some big jobs, in Jesus' name."

He and his wife did that for five months, but nothing happened. In the fifth month he got up off his knees one morning after worshipping God, and the telephone rang.

It was a man from one of those big corporations. "We hear that you have some equipment for the sugar cane fields," the man said. "We would like you to come to our office to talk with us."

When he met with them in their office, they said: "Something happened and we need some extra workers. We have a contract here, and we'll give you $80,000 if you will operate your equipment for us for about six weeks."

He signed the contract, did the work, and collected that amount from them. The whole time, he kept praising the Lord and thanking God for it.

I had told him, "Now when you start getting money, you have got to keep thanking God for it."

Before the six-week job was finished, they called him again and said, "We want to give you another $80,000 contract."

And they did.

"I bow down before God now every day," he said. "I had never done that in my life, but I know God is my Source. Worshipping and praising Him brought me totally out of the hole. After twelve months I paid off that $15,000 debt!

"Today I tithe to my church. Right now I have $40,000 in my savings account and another $80,000 job is coming up after this one."

I talked with the man's pastor the next year when I went to speak at his church, and he said, "Norvel, you taught him what to do, and that man tithed $65,000 to this church last year!"

Now try that on for size! Only a year and a half before, the man couldn't even give his children lunch money. He was totally broke. He was a nice fellow, but he didn't know what to do. He could have just sat there until he died. He might have lost his wife and family along the way. He would have just messed up until somebody came along and told him the truth.

But when he heard the truth, he was willing to act on it. He took time to seek the Lord. He bowed down on his face before God. He spent time worshipping and praising the Lord — and God met him there!

4
God's Covenant With You

4

God's Covenant With You

...he [God] will ever be mindful of his covenant.
Psalm 111:5

One morning when I was in Los Angeles, California, the Spirit of God moved upon me and began to reveal to me about the covenant He has made with His people.

He said, "I have made a covenant with the human race, son. They didn't make it with Me. I made it with them. I'm their God, and they're My children. [Lev. 26:12.] If they will enter into the covenant I've made and be My children, I'll do great and mighty things for them. I will be their God, and they can have anything they want that's in the Bible. But they must worship Me."

Then He said, "I'll prove Myself to you today in the service you are about to go into. Speak on the power there is in praise and the power there is in worship. You just call on Me, and I'll prove it to you. My Word will stand the test. My Word will stand the fire, and so will I."

God's got a gospel that will produce victory, and you'll get the victory through Christ Jesus. Do you understand that? You'll get the victory through prayer and through faith in Him.

You say, "I believe, Brother Norvel. I believe." Yes, you may believe, but the question God is asking the human race is, "Do you believe Me enough to worship Me?"

He went on, "I will prove Myself in this next service by My power through barren women. I want to use them as an example in the service. I could use anyone or anything for an example, but because I want them all to have the victory I will use them. I want them to realize that I promised victory to every human being on earth that will give Me time in praise and give Me time in worship. Any human being, any denomination or any church that will not break the covenant I have made with them can have anything they want."

People everywhere are trying to do this and trying to do that, but they don't spend any time worshipping and praising God. They have a lot of problems and want a bunch of things from God, but they need to enter a different realm of dedication towards God than what they've known. Thank God for all that they already know, but God is saying they need to enter a different realm of dedication, a realm of praise and worship unto God daily.

After God said those things to me about what He wanted to do in that meeting, I did as He said. I asked for all the barren women to come down front, and they did. They began to come and worship God all around the altar in that big church. As we worshipped Him, the Spirit of God came down upon us in a mighty way, and the glory of God filled that sanctuary. God will give barren woman a new womb if she needs one.

A Prophecy on His Covenant

But even before that part of the service, there was a time of real worship and praise. That's when a spirit of prophecy came forth, and the word of the Lord was spoken. You know, when that happens, the Holy Ghost can read your sermon to a congregation. He can tell them your sermon before you've even said a word!

The man who was used by God to share that word of prophecy didn't know anything about what I was going to speak on. I hadn't said anything yet. I hadn't called the barren women down front. I hadn't told them anything about the covenant that God had said He made with the human race. But that was spoken out in prophecy.

I want to share this word from the Lord that the man spoke in that meeting with you. Pay close attention to what He says about His covenant with us.

"As Adam walked with Me in the Garden," says the Spirit of the living God, "so I would have a people who would call out unto Me and cry unto Me and worship Me," saith the Spirit of Grace.

"And as you create the atmosphere of praise and the clouds of glory begin to descend, the Lord thy God shall ride upon the clouds in His majesty and come to visit His people once again."

And the Lord says, "Do not seek for revival and do not look for a breakthrough, but look for the King of kings and look for Me, saith the Spirit, for I Myself shall visit you," saith the Lord.

"I will not send a revival, but I Myself will come, for I am looking and searching throughout the earth," saith the Lord.

"I am looking for a people who will worship Me in spirit and in truth, who will dedicate and consecrate themselves to Me," saith the Lord.

"I am waiting for a generation of people who will come before Me with clean hands and a pure heart, who will worship and serve Me only and bow down to no other god," saith the Lord.

"I am waiting for a people who will cry unto Me and draw nigh unto Me, for I am longing to manifest My glory," saith the Lord, "and let the lightning bolts of My thunder come forth," saith the Spirit.

*"Oh, My people, if you would **make a covenant of praise with Me and make a covenant of worship with Me," saith the Lord,** "even if any shall come up with Me," saith the Spirit, "you shall transcend the law of sin and death," saith the Lord.*

"You shall rise up in My power and glory, and I shall have a people who shall walk in dynamic power, who shall walk with authority," saith the Lord, "for the earth is Mine and the fullness thereof, and it doesn't belong to the Devil. He doesn't own anything," saith the Lord.

*"**So rise up, My people, and enter into a covenant with Me and worship Me," saith the Lord, "and praise Me," saith the Spirit,** "for I have an atmosphere created upon this earth that will drive the demons away," saith the Lord, "that My glory might be revealed.*

"Oh, My people, feel My presence, experience My majesty. For it's a taste of what is to come where I shall pour out My glory in the days ahead, and the finest hour shall come," saith the Lord.

"Therefore, know, and know this surely," saith the Spirit, "you are the people I have chosen, and I have ordained this place to worship Me and to praise Me with My creative power," saith the Spirit of God.

Make a Covenant With God

Now read closely. God made a covenant with the human race.

You *are* human, aren't you?

Then He's made a covenant with you!

But you must choose to worship Him and give Him praise. After hearing a word like that from the Spirit of God, you really need to praise Him and worship Him!

Give the Lord Jesus Christ praise from your lips and from your heart and from your mind. Get words of worship and praise into your thinking; then raise your hands before God, and say this to Him:

"I praise You, Jesus. I love You, Lord. You are my Lord and my God. Blessed be the name of the Lord God forever! I worship You and I praise You, O Lord God. I praise Thy wonderful name. Thank You, Lord. You are the true and living God.

"Oh, God, I make a covenant with You that I will praise the name of Jesus, and I shall worship You all the days that I live.

"Thank You, Lord, for making me strong and not weak. Blessed be the Lord God forever! Oh, I worship You, Jesus, and I praise Your holy name. Thank You, Lord. I worship You and praise You, in Jesus' name."

Make this time of worship a part of you, just like your right arm is a part of you and your left arm is a part of you. Set aside a time of worship and praise unto God. Praise Him for a while; then worship Him. Praise Him and worship Him.

Stay in God's Will

You know, if you don't ever worship God and praise Him, you are, very simply, out of God's will.

"What do you mean, Brother Norvel, when you say we are 'out of God's will'?" You may say, "I go to church and love the Lord. I am not out of God's will."

You may not think so, but you are living beneath your means. You are living afar — far from where you could be living.

"Now that isn't true, Brother Norvel," you may say. "I'm not living afar. I love the Lord. I pray during church. I get blessed in the song service. And I even weep."

But if you only worship during a church service and only get blessed when you sing those songs in church, you are not really worshipping Him the way He wants you to. And you will never be able to enjoy God's best.

You see, if you've not been spending time worshipping God yourself, you've been living your life in the permissive will of God. But all you have to have, my friend, is dedication to come back to Him.

This is your own choice. You have to make the decision to return to God and begin to worship Him.

Then you have a right to pray and ask God for things. If you are trying to pray and ask God for a lot of things without ever worshipping Him, you will usually get a few things just because He loves you so much.

But always remember this: many things you will never get unless you yourself make a covenant with

God. Many of the blessings of God that He has for a
human being — or the human race, or the church — will
never come to you unless you make that covenant of
worship and covenant of praise with Him. Many of
those blessings, you will never get. Never!

"Well, I pray, Brother Norvel," somebody may say.
"But it seems like God doesn't hear me. I try to live my
life clean, Brother Norvel. I love the Lord, and I give my
money to the Gospel. I don't know why God wouldn't
hear me when I pray."

Well, all that sounds good, but it sounds religious,
and that's about what it is. I'm not talking about being
religious. I'm talking about having a relationship with
God.

You might say: "Brother Norvel, I need help. I can't
pay my bills. My body has sickness in it. I'm in terrible
shape! I need Jesus to help me."

We are the church of the Lord Jesus Christ, and Jesus
is Head of the church. If you will just tell God how
much you need His Son to help you, He will. All you
have to do is be willing to give yourself over completely
to God.

Choose To Worship Him

Look at some other Scripture verses about worship
and praise.

**O come, let us worship and bow down: let us kneel
before the Lord our maker.**

Psalm 95:6

**Exalt the Lord our God, and worship at his holy hill;
for the Lord our God is holy.**

Psalm 99:9

Let every thing that hath breath praise the Lord.
Praise ye the Lord.

Psalm 150:6

God's people shall praise and glorify His name forever and ever — for as long as we have breath, as long as we shall live. That is forever and ever!

Praise and glorify God. All the bad things that the Devil has put upon you will disappear, and all your children who are lost will come into the Kingdom of God. All of them. None of your children have any business going to hell, so you just begin to stand in the gap for them yourself. Stand in the gap for them like Ezekiel 22:30 talks about: **I sought for a man among them, that should make up the hedge, and stand in the gap before me....**

Yes, you may be in trouble. Praise and worship God.

You may be broke. I've been broke before, so I know what it is like. Praise and worship God.

You may be sick. I know what that is like, too. When I was a child, I had to stay out of school for one year. I had pleurisy, and they thought I was going to die. I couldn't even breathe the air outside for that whole year. My mother would heat irons and hot water bottles, then put them at my feet, because the doctor said, "If he catches cold, he will die." But I'll have you know I'm alive today!

My Vision of Life Since Birth

While I was in Florida one time, God gave me a vision of the day I was born. The people I was with and

I had been in intercession, and as we were praying, the Spirit of God came all over me, and I fell over on the couch all of a sudden. That is when God began to give me a vision on the wall. It was like a movie screen in front of me.

He let me see myself from the time I was a baby. He showed me everything that had ever happened to me.

Then He said: "This has happened to you because the Devil has been trying to destroy you since the day you were born. But I anointed you, son, before you ever came out of your mother's womb. She gave you to Me, and I had a work for you to do for Me."

That vision made me appreciate what it meant to be loved by God. Every day I thank Him and praise Him and worship Him so much for all that He means to me.

Parents, do like my mother did for me and give your children over to Jesus. Promise God that you will dedicate your children to Him like my mother dedicated me. I promise you, God can meet you there and make a difference in the lives of your kids. If necessary, He will perform a miracle for you — a miracle! It makes no difference what kind of miracle. He can do it if you need one.

Give Yourself Over to Him

Jesus is the miracle worker. He wants you to have God's best. Just remember to worship Him. Why? Because He is worthy of praise and worship.

Rejoice in the Lord, ye righteous; and give thanks at the remembrance of his holiness.

Psalm 97:12

Worship God in His holiness, not in doctrines. Just worship God in His holiness.

Start worshipping the Lord and praising Him, giving yourself over to Him. Start telling Jesus how much you love Him.

Say: "Lord, I give myself totally over to You. My life belongs to You, Jesus. My body belongs to You, Jesus. And, Lord, I give my children over to You."

If you are married but haven't been able to bear children, give that over to Him now. Just start telling Jesus how you feel. Say, "Lord, in Your time I want to bear children." I promise you that God will not leave you barren. You don't have to be barren. Put your eyes on Him as your Provider, and give your future children over to Him. There is no use in waiting until you are expecting a baby. Give that little one over to Him now before you ever conceive it.

Say: "Lord, any offspring of mine are Yours, Jesus, for the Gospel's sake. So, Lord, before I start to carry a baby, I give it to You now."

The Lord God performs miracles like that all the time. It is no problem for Him to do that.

"Well, Brother Norvel, the doctor says there is something wrong with my womb," someone may say.

That doesn't make any difference. The Holy Ghost can give you a new womb if you need one. He can straighten out all your inward parts.

Just keep worshipping the Lord and praising Him; keep talking to Him. The Spirit of God will come upon you and minister to you. The Holy Spirit is precious.

Don't be ashamed. Tell God what you need from Him. Tell Him now, and just throw that need over on Him. Don't you carry it around. You take that need to Him, and let Him have it. You take the undefeated things about your life to Him, and lay them on the altar. Leave them at His feet.

Say this to Him:

"Thank You, Jesus, for loving me. I don't want all these problems, Lord. They are about to drive me nuts, so I give them over to You. I don't want them, and I'm not going to have them, so I just give them to You, Jesus.

"Lord, You take my body and make it new. Take my mind and make it strong. I give my children over to You. I give my job and my business over to You. I am just going to praise You and worship You for as long as I live, in Jesus' name."

Receive the Abundant Life God Has for You

God said He was looking for a people who would establish with Him a covenant of praise and a covenant of worship. He is looking for a people, a church, a human race who would establish and make a covenant with Him. He has already made one and set it before you. And He isn't going to break His covenant. I can tell you that now. We are the ones who have broken the covenant, not God.

If you will make a covenant with God and begin to praise Him and worship Him, you will come on into the abundant life that will set you free. "Will God do it for me?" you may say.

God wants to bless you. He wants to meet all your needs and give you the desires of your heart. Anything that God does for me, He wants to do for you. Anything God does for anybody else, He wants to do for you, too. Understand that!

God will do it for you, but remember: without the covenant of praising His name and worshipping Him, without the covenant going from you to Him, you are breaking the covenant. God wants to bless you abundantly, and Jesus paid the price for you to have those blessings. If you have accepted Jesus but are not keeping the covenant of worship and praise, you won't be receiving the abundant life God wants for you. Oh, you will receive blessings in church, and you will receive some things from God, but there will be many, many things that your life will be lacking. They just will not come your way unless you make that covenant of praise and covenant of worship with Him.

God is looking for people who will make that covenant with Him. God has already made His part of the covenant. He is looking for a people who will take part in it. So enter into the covenant of worship and praise. Open your spirit to God. Set your heart and mind on Him. Give Him all the worship and praise your heart can muster. He is ready to receive it this very moment. Then when you pray, the answers will come. And He'll do great and mighty things for you!

5
When the Flesh Rises Up, Worship God

5

When the Flesh Rises Up, Worship God

Give unto the Lord the glory due unto his name;
worship the Lord in the beauty of holiness.
Psalm 29:2

The sermon you have heard all your life that says you have got to be broke in order to be holy is not in line with the Word. Now it is good for you to be holy. That should be the number one thing in your life. But I know the flesh will rise up and desire things that God doesn't want us to have. I live in a body with flesh, too.

Sometimes there are certain things that you might like to have, things that everybody likes, but you can't always have them. You know you want them. Sometimes you want them "real bad." But God says you can't have them. When He says that, you just have to say *no* to them and walk away.

The greatest word you can ever say to temptation is *No!*

The greatest word you can ever say to the Devil is *No!*

The greatest word you can ever say against a particular desire in your life is just plain *No!*

You just have to say *No!* That's all!

The Devil understands the word *No.*

When he says to you, "Try this," or, "Do this," you just have to say, *NO!*

Then he'll say, "But you know you want to do it, so just go ahead."

What do you say?

NO!

I Said, "No!"

One morning my doorbell rang. When I opened the door, a tall, slim, beautiful blond woman was standing there.

After she walked in to my house, I said, "What do you want?"

"I've come to get you," she said.

"What do you mean you've come to get me?"

"Well, you're a bachelor, aren't you?"

"Oh, yes."

"Well," she said, "I know you get lonely. I've come to fulfill that loneliness." Naturally, with her saying that, I knew she wasn't a Christian.

I said, "Oh, really?"

"Yes," she said. "I know that since you're a bachelor you're bound to get lonely. Aren't you normal?"

"Oh, yes, I'm normal all right."

"Well, I've come to fulfill that desire."

"Young lady, you just have to understand something about me. I'm probably just as normal as you are, but I can't have both you and Jesus. And I don't want to trade Jesus for you!"

"What? What did you say?"

"I said, 'I can't have both you and Jesus. And I don't want to trade Jesus for you.'"

"I don't know why," she said. "You can have us both. You've already got Him, and now here I am."

But I said, "No! No!"

"You know you want to. You're a bachelor. Well, here I am."

But I just kept saying, "No!...No!...No!" I stood right there until I had talked her out of it.

If you try to get people like that saved, they won't attack you. You have to start talking to them about how much Jesus loves them.

I didn't say to her, "You creep, get out of my house!"

I said, "Well, I'm sure a pretty girl like you won't have any trouble finding a man. You're so pretty. But I can't do that. I just can't."

You have to be careful when you are talking to a person like her. If you do anything wrong, you might make her mad. And there is no telling what she might say about you then!

There are a lot of women like that. I go to lots of meetings, and there are lots of people in the hotels and convention centers and churches. Most of the time these women don't know where I am staying, but sometimes they do.

Sometimes I will see a lady in a meeting. Then when I walk through the hotel lobby, I see her sitting there. I try to look the other way. Then I go straight to my room and don't come out!

Worship Over Desire

After a meeting one night, I was walking through the hotel lobby. The fellow with me said: "Hey, Norvel, there's that beautiful girl I saw in the meeting tonight. She was sitting on the front row. Did you see her?"

"Oh, yes. I guess everybody saw her. She was so dressed up."

"Well, she's sitting right there. Don't you want to go over and talk to her?"

"No, I don't! But let me teach you something about a situation like this." (She was sitting close to the elevator, and it was hard to keep from seeing her.)

Then I said to him: "As we walk to the elevator, be careful not to glance over toward her. Let's just keep talking and get on the elevator as soon as possible."

So we talked and talked and talked. After I had pushed the button, the elevator doors opened, and we got on it as quickly as we could and headed up to the room.

"Now, young man, get into your room. The only way you can keep away from a pretty girl like that is by staying in your room.

"Don't let the Devil tell you, 'Go to the lobby and get a paper.' Don't let him talk you into going back downstairs for any reason. That is exactly what he will try to do. If you say *no* to him, he will try coming at you from some other angle, anything he can to get you into the lobby, so that you will start talking to her.

"Don't go downstairs. Just stay in your room. Don't even answer the phone. Just put your eyes on God and start worshipping the Lord. Get down on the floor and worship Him. Just worship Him more and more."

Watch Your Associations

I am not smart in myself. I dropped out of school. I am not supposed to have any sense. But because of God, I am prosperous. He has blessed me beyond belief!

Not too long ago, I put a piece of my property up for sale. I had paid $90,000 for it, but I was offered much more than that.

People may ask, "How much are you worth, Brother Norvel?"

I really don't know. I have no earthly idea. I don't even keep track of it, and couldn't care less. I just live the simple life, just as simple as I can.

I have already been involved with the country club and the fancy bunch and found out they are as phony as the Devil. I don't want to get involved anymore with wealthy socialites.

At home in Cleveland, Tennessee, they have tried to get me to join all the country clubs and go to all the social functions with all the "successful" people. I hide from them! I don't even want to go around them.

If I stayed around places like that, all the neglected wives would want attention. Because they need someone to care, they will reach out for a man they think can fill their wants and desires. I know that kind of thing is going to happen before I ever go, and I don't want to get involved in that.

My God, deliver me from that kind of a world! Dear Jesus, help us all! I just want to be plain and simple before God. I want to worship the Lord and praise His name because I know that the blessings of God will come on me as I keep my eyes on Him.

Don't Let Pride Stand in the Way

One time I spoke at this great, big, fancy banquet in Georgia. When I got through speaking, I gave an altar call. When you get a thousand invitations, it doesn't matter whether they invite you back or not. So while you're there, you may as well give an altar call and get some folks blessed.

When I finished giving the altar call, about two hundred people got out of their seats and walked down to the front. One of the businessmen who had come forward had a wife who had received the baptism of the Holy Spirit. She had knelt down before the Lord in their bedroom by the bed and prayed and said, "Jesus, please baptize me in the Holy Spirit." And He baptized her in the Holy Spirit. The heavenly language began to come up out of her, and she began to speak it out so beautifully and gloriously. It was so precious.

Her husband was stubborn and said that he didn't believe in that kind of stuff. After a while, she just kept on loving him and would pray in English and speak out in her heavenly language some. He got used to seeing her beside the bed praying, and he would just lie there and watch her.

Finally he got to the point that he was convinced it was real and was even wanting it himself. But he was full of pride, and he told God, "God, I believe in that now, and I want You to give that to me. I want You to give it to me the same way my wife got it — in private, on my knees, by my bed, where no one can see me.

There were about two thousand people at the banquet the day he decided to come forward. Everything was really sweet and nice until all of a sudden someone slammed up against the wall and just hung there. When I looked over, there this businessman was. He was trying to push himself up while he was sliding down the wall saying, "Oh, no God, no, not in front of all these people. My wife didn't get it like this." He would pull himself up again then God's power would push him down again, and he would be speaking in tongues.

When God got through with him, he didn't have any pride left. All the pride he had was exposed, and he knew he was a meathead. If you ever in your life try to tell God anything, it is for sure that He will never do it that way. Believe me, this may be a shock to you, but God knows a lot more than you know. And because He is God, He can't afford to let you tell Him anything. You ask Him for what you want when it's promised to you in the Bible, and then you step back and let God do it the way He wants to do it.

But don't go around full of pride like this man did and say, "God, I'm a classy man, and I want what my wife has because it's so beautiful. But I want You to give it to me quietly. I don't want anybody to know that I speak in tongues. So give it to me in my bedroom. Do You understand me?"

Of course, God doesn't even answer people like that. Oh, He understood him all right, and He knew exactly how to make him look like an ox in a china shop. He was the most miserable looking mess I had ever seen in my life. But he got the baptism of the Holy Spirit and started speaking in tongues. And he won't ever forget it.

No Blue Mondays!

Some people's emotions get the best of them, and they live from day to day on a roller coaster. One day they are up, and one day they are down. God told me this about that kind of life. He said: "Son, I don't have any blue Mondays. What are *you* doing with them?"

"Well, Lord, if You don't believe in them, then I won't believe in them either. Praise God! I'm going to worship You all during that blue Monday."

"Son, I don't believe in blue Mondays or gray Tuesdays."

"Then neither do I!"

Whenever you find out how Jesus believes about something, then agree with Him as quickly as you can. Just say, "I'm going to believe like that, too, Jesus." As long as you try your best to follow after Him, your mistakes will become fewer and fewer.

During meetings and conventions, I fellowship with my brothers and sisters in the Lord, but I can hardly wait sometimes until the service starts the next morning. When I am speaking in those morning sessions, I always get anointed really strong because I spent time worshipping the Lord. If you will take time to worship God, your life will be like that every day — *every day*!

Sometimes I have ridden in the van with my ministry team on the way to another city for a meeting. As we listen to anointed music tapes, we just worship God and praise His name. That is when I get blessed. Something blesses me, and I just want to keep praising God over and over again!

If you are living a dead, dry life and you are wondering about God, you may say: "My life doesn't seem very exciting. What do you think is wrong with me, Brother Norvel?"

I probably wouldn't have enough time to tell you all that is wrong with you, but I know about something that will help pull you out. I can guarantee you that. It will totally get you out of what is wrong with you.

The next time your flesh rises up and you start to have a bad day or a confused day or a blue day, start worshipping God and praising Him. Tell Jesus how much you love Him. Thank Him for all He has done for you. Praise Him for caring enough to give His own life on the cross two thousand years ago. Begin to really worship Him and praise Him.

Notice the second verse in Psalm 29. It says:

Give unto the Lord the glory due unto his name; worship the Lord in the beauty of holiness.

Give unto the Lord the glory that is due unto His name. That is truly worshipping the Lord!

Have you done that lately?

"But, Brother Norvel," someone may say, "I go to church."

Rats and mice go to church, too!

"Well, I got saved years ago, Brother Norvel, and I love the Lord."

Are you singing the same song over and over again? Are you saying, "I love the Lord...I love the Lord...I love the Lord!" over and over again like a habit?

Just going to church or saying, "I love the Lord" over and over isn't worshipping God. You are to worship God for His name and His power. You are to worship Him all the time — all the time — in the beauty of holiness. As you do, your outlook on your everyday life will change. You will expect God's blessings to come on you because you are keeping your eyes on Him, and you won't have any more blue Mondays!

6
What To Do When You Are Desperate

6

What To Do When
You Are Desperate

*. . . and when he saw him, he fell at his feet,
and besought him greatly. . . .*

Mark 5:22,23

How on God's green earth do you ever get the God
that made the whole world to hear you and to respond
to you when you are in a desperate situation? There is a
way. And when you learn that way, you will save your
life and your children's lives too.

There was a fellow some years back who was
desperate because his daughter was dying. He knew
Jesus had the answer. And whether you know it or not,
He has the answer for you, and you're desperate for that
answer. This fellow loved God, trusted in God and
believed in God so much that He was willing to fall on
his knees and bow down before Jesus in the middle of a
crowd. He was desperate for God to find favor with him.

Fall at Jesus' Feet

If you're like this fellow and are desperate for God to
find favor with you, turn to Mark, chapter 5, verse 22.

**And, behold, there cometh one of the rulers of the
synagogue, Jairus by name; and when he saw him, he fell
at his feet.**

75

Now, let me teach you something here. Anything that you ever see a human being doing to Jesus when He was ministering on earth in person, you can do. You can get the same results by doing the same thing now by faith.

God is a faith God. By grace you are saved through faith. (Eph. 2:8.) By the mercy of God through faith, you are healed. Because of your faith in God, He will perform miracles in your life.

You could say, "But Norvel, Jesus was there in person." It doesn't matter. You can do the same thing by faith today. That is what the church is all about. You have a right to come to the altar and get it.

You can't sit there in your seat and be full of pride and expect to get something from God. You have to come God's way. God likes you to come publicly. He likes to watch you walk down the aisle and bow down on your knees before Him at the altar. He likes to put his power on the inside of you. He likes to put his arms around you and love you like you've never been loved in all of your life.

I tell boys in the penitentiary all the time, "Look, lust and greed and whiskey and women and dope put you in here, but if I can talk you into giving your life to Jesus and getting filled with the Holy Spirit, He will take you on a trip so high that you'll throw rocks at L.S.D."

So get rid of your pride and come to God His way. Jairus did.

Believe Jesus Will Help You

Now notice, after Jairus fell at Jesus' feet, he believed Jesus would help him. Look at what he says in verse 23.

And besought him greatly, saying, My little daughter lieth at the point of death: I pray thee, come and lay thy hand on her, that she may be healed; and she shall live.

If you were God what would you do? I would do the same thing Jesus did. If I were Jesus and were walking along like this and some man approached me and came and fell at my feet and said, "My little girl lies at home at the point of death. Please come and lay Your hands on her, and she will live and not die," I think I would listen.

I don't know all about God, but I know quite a bit about Him, and I'm telling you that I have never known Him to turn anybody away who did that. Never! Not one time have I ever seen Jesus turn away anybody that worshipped and bowed down before Him in reverence asking Him for help. He didn't turn me away. He didn't turn my daughter Zona away.

She had been on dope for three years, and I had been praying for three years, but she wouldn't listen to me or any other human being. Then one day, God sent an angel, and she listened to the angel. I can tell you that! She hasn't taken any dope since.

God has His own way of doing things. In the Old Testament, a man's hand wrote some words on the king's palace wall during a party, and everyone went, "Aaahhh." God did what He said He was going to do, and the king and his kingdom were judged. (Dan. 5.) When you're dealing with God, you're dealing with a true Being that spoke the world into existence and has all knowledge. Believe me, your case is not too hard for Him.

When Bad News Comes, Only Believe

So Jesus went with the man to his house. On the way a woman reached out in faith and touched His clothes and was healed. While Jesus was talking to this woman, a man came running up from Jairus' house with some bad news. He said to Jairus:

> . . . Thy daughter is dead: why troublest thou the Master any further?
>
> **verse 35**

Do you know what Jesus said to Jairus? He said:

> . . . Be not afraid, only believe.
>
> **verse 36**

And Jesus kept walking towards the house. This man had come and fallen at Jesus's feet and told Him, "I believe in You. I believe if You'll come and pray for my daughter that she'll live and not die. I bow myself down before You, Jesus. I worship You, Jesus. If You'll come pray for my daughter, she'll live and not die. She will live."

And Jesus said, "Well, I will," and went with the man, and the daughter died while they were on their way. And Jesus said, "Don't be afraid. Only believe." And He kept on walking, full of faith, full of power, full of knowledge. Death didn't scare Him. He kept on walking.

Refuse To Be Intimidated by People

When He got there, there were people all around crying, and He said to them:

> . . . Why make ye this ado, and weep? the damsel is not dead, but sleepeth.

And they laughed him to scorn. But when he had put them all out, he taketh the father and the mother of the damsel, and them that were with him, and entereth in where the damsel was lying.

And he took the damsel by the hand, and said unto her, Talitha cumi; which is, being interpreted, Damsel, I say unto thee, arise.

And straightway the damsel arose, and walked; for she was of the age of twelve years. And they were astonished with a great astonishment.

And he charged them straitly that no man should know it; and commanded that something should be given her to eat.

verses 39-43

So there was Jesus. When He arrived, people were crying. When He told them she was only sleeping, they began to laugh at Him. But He didn't pay any attention to them, and He took that father and that mother into the room where their daughter was and took her by the hand and lifted her up. Then He told them to get her something to eat. Even death can't hold back the power of God!

Now why would God do something like that for a human being? Because he had found favor with Him.

Stop Your Unbelieving Crying and Begging

"Well, now, Brother Norvel, I've seen cases like that before, and God didn't do anything for them," you may say.

Wait a minute. God doesn't do anything for anybody unless that person finds favor with Him. Did that person find favor with Him? I know of cases where God didn't do anything either. They're crying and begging and crying and begging God to do something, but they're full of unbelief, and God hardly does anything for them.

They need to stop their crying and begging and come to the altar, get on their knees and say, "I believe. I'm not afraid. I believe. I call my child well. I'm not afraid. I believe. The God I serve is real. I worship You, Jesus. I worship You, Jesus. My daughter will live and not die. In the name of the Lord Jesus Christ, I worship You and bow down before You."

Stop your unbelieving crying and begging. We've all been taught the same way, every last one of us. A member of the family dies, and the family begins to faint and fall on the floor and cry. The only One Who doesn't do that is Jesus.

Sure, your natural heart is broken. You loved that person. I understand. My mother died when I was nine years old, and I cried for about two years. But nobody in the church even said to me, "Jesus loves her just like you did. Let's bow down right here around the bed and worship Him." No one started out in worship and said, "We worship You, Jesus, and we want our mother, Lord. We worship You, Jesus. You're our God. Glory to You, God. Thank You for Thy power and Thy glory. We worship You, Jesus. We bow down before You, Jesus. We worship You, Jesus. We believe in the Lord God of the New Testament. In Jesus' name we worship You."

We did nothing like that! When you don't do it the Bible way, you don't get Bible results. When you do it the natural way, you get natural results. That is all you'll ever get. It's that simple. It's just that simple.

Beseech Him Greatly

Why does God want me to teach you this? Because the next time that the devil comes and tries to knock you for a loop or one of your children gets into a car wreck and the doctors tell you that they don't know if he will live or not or some goofy thing happens to you, He wants you to know what to do.

Don't come unglued. Don't start walking the floor, wringing your hands saying, "God, what did this happen to me for?" No, say, "In Jesus' name, I bind you Satan. Take your hands off my child. In the name of the Lord Jesus Christ I claim God's power to come upon my child's body. Wherever he is right now, in Jesus' name, let Your mighty power come upon his body so he will live and not die." Then walk the floor and pray in the Spirit. Pray victory. Pray in the Spirit.

I had to do that a while back one night for about an hour in my house. When I got the long distance call from Texas nobody was at the house but a pastor friend of mine and me. An Assembly of God pastor from Dallas, Texas, had just had a heart attack.

We hit the floor and started praying as hard and as fast as we could. If we had waited a few moments, he could have died. I mean we started praying as hard and as fast as we could for about an hour, "Satan, you're not going to kill that Assembly of God pastor. I bind you in Jesus' name. Let him go free. Thank You, Lord, for Your mighty power. Thank You, Lord, for going into that room and touching him right now."

After about an hour, the glory of God came into that room. My pastor friend fell over on the couch under the power of God and began to prophesy. God told us that we had prayed correctly.

If you ever find yourself in a desperate situation, pray hard and fast. Let the devil know you're on the scene. Break the power of the devil over them in English, in the name of Jesus, then immediately start praying in tongues, in the Spirit, until you pray yourself right on over into the spirit world where you can reach victory.

There was no hope for him. He had just had a massive heart attack. But after an hour of praying in Jesus' name and claiming his health in Jesus' name, God healed his heart. God will heal your heart, too. He can pump a new heart into your chest just that quickly. The Lord can give you your eyesight just that quickly. Jesus can give you a new kidney so quickly it will make your head swim.

There is only one Jesus, friend. You may have been misinformed up until this point, but now you know the truth, and the truth will set you free. The truth will make you well.

Get in Shape for Prayer
by Worshipping Him

The Lord also said to me one day: "The person who will come before Me to praise and worship Me will get himself in shape to enter into the world of prayer."

For the most part, the church is not in shape. All they want to do in prayer is beg God to do something for them or argue with Him about something. I'm telling you right now that it's a waste of energy and a waste of breath. There's no reason to go to God in prayer and agonize with Him over and over and over again.

First of all you establish a lifestyle of praising His name and worshipping Him. Then you go to Him in prayer. Do you understand that? There is a way to get your prayers answered, every one of them. It isn't hard to get your prayers answered. There is an easy way.

If you're dying with a disease, you can get your prayer answered, and the healing power of God will come into you and drive out affliction, just totally drive it out. But you're going to have to pay the price. You are going to have to make your own covenant with God and make a commitment to worship Him daily. You're going to have to make it a way of living.

If you'll establish a covenant with Him, if you'll praise Him and worship Him, He will become your God all the time in every situation.

Your Victory Will Come

Sometimes in life you have these great big situations, these great big mountains to fly up over. You don't know how to handle it. That's okay because He does. Don't worry about it.

Just get on your knees and praise Him and worship Him for a while; then bind up the devil and pray in tongues for about thirty minutes or an hour, and bless God, I guarantee you that victory will hit you like a bolt of lightning.

All of a sudden it will become like a teeny, little thing. It won't have any meaning anymore. Do you know why those circumstances look so big in front of you? It's because you don't have a covenant with God. You don't have a covenant of praise and worship, and you're trying to figure things out in your own natural mind.

You can't do it, not if you want to live by faith. You've got to flip that mess over on God. I don't care what it is. Throw it over on the Lord. Make a covenant with Him and begin to praise and worship Him, and I'll guarantee you that God is big enough to get the miracle for you that you need.

Do you understand what I'm saying to you? Get a glimpse of what I'm telling you. If you can just get a little glimpse of it and throw that great need you have over onto God, instead of trying to drive yourself nuts, God will do a miracle for you.

You say to yourself, "I'm going to do it by myself. I'll do it myself. I'm so beaten down I think I'll go to Florida for a vacation. Maybe all I need is a vacation."

It's all right to go to Florida and walk the beaches for a while and listen to the waves. That's all right. But there isn't any reason for you to be beaten down when you go. Throw your need over on God and worship Him; then go.

Remember, there's only one Jesus, and that's the One you find in Matthew, Mark, Luke and John. There is not another One. That's the only One there is, and He is saying to the whole human race, "Come and follow Me."

7
Add Faith To Your Worship

7

Add Faith To Your Worship

Then Jesus answered and said unto her, O woman, great is thy faith: be it unto thee even as thou wilt.

Matthew 15:28

Our God is a God Who speaks things into existence by faith. He waits for us to do the same and blesses everybody on earth according to what He hears from them. Today, there are things that are lacking in some people's lives because they have failed to act in faith.

You may be saying to yourself, "I basically love God, but all these crazy, squirrely things keep happening to me all the time. I don't like living in a world like this. Can you help me?"

A Cry for Mercy

Let's start with a Scripture that God showed me so you will see it for yourself. It begins in Matthew 15:

Then Jesus went thence, and departed into the coasts of Tyre and Sidon.

And, behold, a woman of Canaan came out of the same coasts, and cried unto him, saying, Have mercy on me, O Lord, thou son of David; my daughter is grievously vexed with a devil.

verses 21,22

This woman had a devil-possessed daughter, demon-possessed. This woman had heard about Jesus. She was a Gentile woman who had come crying, asking for mercy. Notice the beginning of the next verse.

> **But he answered her not a word. And his disciples came and besought him, saying, Send her away; for she crieth after us.**
>
> **But he answered and said, I am not sent but unto the lost sheep of the house of Israel.**
>
> verses 23,24

Jesus wouldn't even talk to her. Why? Because her approach was wrong. She was failing to put first things first. Today that's the very reason many believers don't have their problems answered either. That's the reason they have a disease, and they've had it for months and months. That's the reason their children are still devil-possessed and they've been that way for a long time. And those children will probably stay that way and go to hell if their parents don't change. Does this apply to you?

"But, Brother Norvel, I love the Lord, and I'm Spirit filled."

Jesus loves you too, but He knows if you're a flake or not. Even if you're saved, Spirit filled, and love God, He won't talk to you much because you fail to put first things first.

At one time in my life, I had no earthly idea that Jesus was even like that. I always thought Jesus walked around really softly and talked softly all the time. In the Sunday school rooms they always had a picture of Jesus sitting there with the little lambs and children around Him. I thought that whatever I wanted to do or say was all right. I didn't have to worry about it because Jesus loved me. Jesus did love me, but if I failed to put first things first, He wouldn't talk to me very much. It's what I call getting a total blank. It's what I call praying for something for years and never receiving it.

Jesus' disciples even came over to Him and wanted to send the woman with the devil-possessed daughter away. They were wild. Do you remember in the Bible where blind Bartemaus began to cry out to Jesus for mercy? Even the crowd told him to be quiet. (Luke 18:39.) Sometimes the disciples were like you and me. They weren't completely with it.

I've got news for you. The Lord Jesus Christ is not like you or me or Peter or Paul or that pastor or evangelist you know. He doesn't think like we do. We're supposed to think like He does. And once you get to know Jesus, you'll find out something really quickly: He is not interested in sending people away if they need help, but He is interested in teaching them the truth because He knows the truth will make them free if they believe it. (John 8:32.) If you don't believe it, you can remain as you are, but if you believe it, it will make you totally free.

She Begins To Worship

Now this woman loved the Lord with all her heart. She loved Him as much as you do, but her approach wasn't working. Jesus Himself wouldn't talk to her. So she said to herself, "I had better change."

If you're not getting victory, then you had better change. God isn't going to change. He remains the same all the time. Through divorce He remains the same.

Through cancer He remains the same. Through demon possession He remains the same. You may climb up mountains and fall into valleys, but God never changes. If you're not getting victory, then you change. Now notice what she does in the next verse:

> **Then came she and worshipped him, saying, Lord, help me.**
>
> **verse 25**

She changed her approach. This time she began to worship Him. She wasn't asking Him, "Why don't You help me? Why don't You have mercy on me?" Don't come whimpering to Him all the time, telling Him all your troubles. He already knows all your troubles. Spend your time with Him worshipping Him.

When was the last time you went before the Lord and just began to worship Him? I worship Jesus lying down, standing up, walking, riding in my car. I worship Him morning, noon and night. I make my worship of Him a way of life.

Just sit there in your living room sometime and begin to worship the Lord. "Won't my family think I'm strange?" you may ask. If you've never done it before, they will. But if you'll do it morning, noon and night for about two or three months, they won't think it's strange. Besides, people who worship Jesus aren't strange. It's the people who don't worship Him that are. You're supposed to worship Jesus. It's normal.

She Continues To Worship

Notice, in verse 26, God puts the woman through a test. He wants to know if she is really sincere and really believes.

But he answered and said, It is not meet to take the children's bread, and to cast it to dogs.

verse 26

In those days Gentile people were known as dogs in the eyes of Jews. It doesn't sound too good. I've seen some flaky dogs, and I've seen some cute dogs, but I don't even want to be called a cute dog. But that is what Jesus said. He called her a dog!

And she said, Truth, Lord: yet the dogs eat of the crumbs which fall from their masters' table.

verse 27

In other words she was saying, "I know you Jews aren't supposed to have anything to do with us Gentiles. I know that you look upon us as dogs, but I only know one thing. You are my Master, and I love You. Even the dogs eat the crumbs from their Master's table."

What did she mean? Well, you could put it this way: "Jesus, without You I am a worm. Without You I am no better than a crumb. Without You I am nothing. My life belongs to You, Jesus. I'll do anything for You, and I'll worship You for the rest of my life. I love You so much that I'll take a crumb of anything You have. You are my Master."

When He looked down on her and saw her keep on worshipping Him and telling Him, "I'll eat all the crumbs I can get," Jesus was so impressed. Her truth and sincerity moved Him.

Her Daughter Is Made Whole

Then Jesus answered and said unto her, O woman, great is thy faith: be it unto thee even as thou wilt. And her daughter was made whole from that very hour.

verse 28

Can you imagine Jesus telling a human being that she has great faith? If God had told me I had faith to please Him, it would so thrill me I couldn't stand it. I would probably run around the block. If Jesus were to tell me I had great faith, I would probably turn a flip in the middle of the air.

"What did He tell her that for?" you may say. "What had she done?"

It's called putting first things first. Have you been putting first things first lately? Have you been worshipping God? Let me tell you something. When you put first things first, you'll not only be healed, but you'll hold on to your healing. When you put first things first, your devil-possessed children will be saved because the Spirit of God will sweep into where they're living and drive all the devils out of them.

When Jesus said, **'O woman, great is thy faith: be it unto thee even as thou wilt,** the Spirit of God went to the village where the demon-possessed daughter was and began to drive out all the devils. When the mother got home, the daughter was completely whole. The woman couldn't have been too far away because evidently she got home within sixty minutes. The Bible says within sixty minutes the daughter was made completely whole.

Everything was done by the Spirit of God because a mother was on her knees, worshipping Jesus and refusing to quit. *She refused to quit.* She was determined to worship Him.

My Daughter Was Made Whole

If you'll worship Jesus every day and sell out to Him, I guarantee you that the Spirit of God will go visit your children and drive the devils out of them. I'm a perfect example. I ought to know because for three years my daughter was on dope, and I couldn't get her off. She wouldn't listen to me or any other human being. I was just crying out and praying for mercy for my daughter. Why? Because she already had five or six little friends that had been buried in Cleveland, Tennessee, because of overdosing.

Every time the phone would ring the devil would say, "It's about her. She's dead." I would say, "No, she's not dead. In Jesus' name stop it, Satan. I break your power over Zona. I command you to take your hands off of her and let her go free." I would walk the floor and say, "Satan, you'll never send my daughter to hell because I'm praying for her in Jesus' name. I'm praying that God's power will go visit her wherever she is at, Playmate Club or wherever.

I prayed for three years, and one night she looked up at the ceiling of the Playmate Club and all of a sudden part of the ceiling turned into my face, and she jumped up and ran out of there.

That supernatural experience along with the angel who visited her in her room were enough to scare the devil out of her. This angel that God sent was about as big as two men. When you're as big as two men and you've just come from heaven, you have the glory of God on you, and you don't have to preach any sermons. You don't have to sing any songs. You don't have to say any prayers. All you have to do is appear.

That angel appeared, and my daughter said, "Aaahhh!" and from that day to this she hasn't taken any more dope. God has His own way of doing things. He spoke the world into existence, and He has all knowledge. His ways may be a little different from yours, but believe me, your case is not too hard for Him.

But you need to learn to put first things first. Sure you need to love God. The woman with the demon-possessed daughter loved God from the very beginning or she wouldn't have been looking for Jesus. If you love Jesus and believe He has the answer for you, you had better be looking for Him. She was looking for Him. She had faith in Him. She loved Him. And she found Him, but she made the wrong approach.

She didn't put first things first. All some people say is, "Give me, give me, give me, Jesus. I'm in trouble, Lord. I'm sorry. Give me, give me, give me." If you think like that, I've got news for you. Jesus is not a give-me Jesus all the time. Jesus' heart overflows with an abundance of joy when He sees you bow down before Him and worship Him.

Put First Things First

You may need a blessing from God. You can have it, but you must put first things first. You must worship Him. Speak His name out of your mouth. It's what comes out of your mouth that defiles you, not the things that go in. Let worship come out of your mouth. Say, "Jesus, I worship You. I love You." Don't ask Him for anything right now. Just worship Him first. Sometimes the Spirit of God will come upon you and heal you even before you ask. God knows what you have need of even before you ask. (Matt. 6:8.) Your child may have been saved while you were worshipping Him.

Remember you can start and stop worshipping Jesus any time you want to. Don't wait until the Spirit of God comes upon you to worship Him. Don't worship Him based upon your feelings. Worship Him because He is God. Worship Him because He died on the cross so you could be saved. Worship Him because He is the Lord of your life.

When you put first things first, then you have a right to ask God for anything. "Well, Brother Norvel," someone may say, "I don't know about that. I ask Him whenever I want to."

That is what the woman thought: "I have a devil-possessed daughter. I'll just go ask Him." But He wouldn't even talk to her. Her first approach didn't work because she failed to put first things first.

If your approach to God is not working and you're not getting healed and your children aren't getting saved, then change your approach. You love Him, and He knows you love Him, but some of you haven't been worshipping Him enough, and you're cutting off the blessing.

God says in 3 John 4, **I have no greater joy than to hear that my children walk in truth.** And when they do, they'll get a blessing from heaven. He wants to give it to you. He wants His power to shoot into Los Angeles. He wants His power to go into New York City and deliver that child of yours.

"Brother Norvel, do you think if I'm faithful to worship Jesus that His power will go to my child and run all the devils out?" someone may say.

Are you kidding? What did He say? I can't tell you that God is going to do it in sixty minutes or less. You can't put God on a time clock. He might take five minutes or five weeks. You can't tell God or anybody else when God is going to do something. God imparts a lot of information to human beings, but He usually doesn't tell when He is going to do something. If He does, it's a supernatural manifestation just for them, but He usually doesn't.

When you put first things first, you have a right to ask Him to save your child. You have a right to ask Him to heal you and set you free. You have a right to have your home back together again.

Ask According to His Will

Once you've shown God that you're interested in believing the Scripture and worshipping Him, then you have a right to ask God for anything according to His will and be bold about it. (1 John 5:14,15.) Open up your mouth. Talk out loud. Ask God for whatever you want — healing, salvation. Go ahead. Ask Him in Jesus' name. Ask in English, not in tongues. Ask Him for what you want. "Jesus, I ask You to save little Tommy. I ask you to save Elizabeth. Jesus, I ask You to allow Your healing power to flow through me. I need to be healed, Jesus."

Jesus plainly told you and me, **Whatsoever ye shall ask the Father in my name, he will give it you** (John 16:23). Why? Because the Father loves the name of Jesus. The Father loves His Son. His Son is the One Who came to earth and paid the sacrificial price that you and I may be saved.

Continue To Worship

If you want to please God Almighty, the Creator of all the universe, if you want to please Him, worship Jesus; have faith in Him.

When you worship Jesus, He will walk into the throne room and say, "Father, that woman down there who is sick and has a devil-possessed child has been worshipping Me."

"How long has she been doing it?" God might say.

"She's been doing it for a week," Jesus might say.

"She might just be doing it to get Me to manifest Myself because they need help but aren't really sincere in worshipping Me. I'm not interested in that game," God might answer.

A month later Jesus may go back and say, "Father, that woman I told You about last month is still worshipping Me, and she tells Me every day that they love You and that they love the Holy Spirit, and they worship Me morning, noon and night."

God the Father could say, and probably does, "I think she might really be sincere, but time will tell."

Time will always bring out the truth. Anybody can have patience with God for a week. Anybody can put up a front for a month. Anybody can stretch their imagination and go to church for three or four months. But, remember, God won't buy those phony tricks. He already knows those tricks. God will give a test. He wants to see how long the person will worship Him. The key is *don't give up.* Just keep on.

Finally the Son will say to the Father, "I have come to make intercession for that family that lives in Nashville, Tennessee, the Smith family. They have a demon-possessed child, and the devil is trying to kill their child, but they've made up their minds to turn their child over to Me. They've made up their minds to turn their family over to Me. They've made up their minds to turn their lives over to Me."

Some people have been born again twenty years, but they've never turned their lives over to Jesus. It's one thing to give your heart to Jesus, but it's another thing to give your life to him.

People give their hearts to Jesus because of conviction or because of a sermon or because they want to stay out of hell. But there is a vast difference in giving your heart to Jesus so you can go to heaven when you die and laying your life down for Him right now while you're rich, sharp and healthy, and the world wants everything you've got. Say to the world, "No, you can't have me. I'm turning my life completely over to Jesus."

Give Him Your Life

God wants your life. He doesn't just want your heart. He will take your heart if that is all you'll give Him, but He wants your life, your substance. If you don't turn your money over to God, your life doesn't belong to God. Your life belongs to your pocketbook. If your life really belonged to God, you would throw it down for Him and give Him anything you've got.

When I go out to a house to get the devil out of a child or pray for them because they're dying, I always ask them two questions. The first question I ask them is, "Do you worship God in this house?"

Nearly everyone will tell me, "We go to church."

I say, "I didn't ask you that. Do you worship Jesus in this house?"

"Uh, Mr. Hayes, we've been church members for a long time, and we've loved God for a long time."

"I didn't ask you that. Do you worship Jesus in this house?"

I already know by now that they don't because if they had they would have said, "Glory to God, yes! We worship God in this house all the time."

Then I ask them, "Do you tithe?"

"Let me tell you what I think about tithing."

"I didn't come here for you to preach to me. I don't even want to know what you think about it. Tell me. Do you tithe?"

"Well, this is my idea."

"I'm not interested in your idea. Do you tithe?"

"Well, no."

"Now let me get this straight. You don't worship Jesus, and you don't tithe, and you want me to come into your house and try to talk God into healing her? Is that right?"

"Yes, that's right."

"Then show Him you believe in Him. Show Him you love Him. Worship Him and pay your tithe.

Thank God in Faith

Now there is one more thing you need to remember. Whatever you thank God for that's in the Bible before you see it, God will let you see it. He will give it to you. That's why God tells you in His Word to give Him thanks in everything. (1 Thess. 5:18.)

Thank God for a good wife. Thank God for a good husband. Thank God for peace in your home. Thank God for your children's being saved. Thank God for a good church. Thank God for your healing.

Now if you have given thanks to God, I have good news for you. If you are a pastor, make special note of this. I'm going to give you a perfect definition of faith. I'm going to let you know exactly what faith is. Anything you can thank God for out loud before you see it Jesus will let you see it. Faith is not seen. You have to thank God for it before you see it. Thank God for what you asked Him for out loud.

Say, "thank You, Lord, for my healing. Thank You, Lord, because Your presence is in my house. Thank You, Jesus, for saving Elizabeth, Tommy and John. Thank You for putting my home back together."

The next time your child, say his name is "John," sasses you and slams the door, walk in his room and hold up your hands and worship God in his room. Confess with your mouth, "The spirit of respect from God will go into my son, John. He will not slam doors and say smart things to me." Then go kneel by his bed and worship God. Lay your hands on his pillow. Say, "When he sleeps in this bed, let the Spirit of peace come into him. Let the Spirit of respect come upon him." You would be surprised what the Holy Ghost will do with him.

All of a sudden, it won't be too long — maybe a week or two — before he'll come up to you and say, "Mother, I'm sorry that I slammed the door and said a smart word to you last week. I've been feeling so bad because I talked to you that way. Will you please forgive me?"

Of course you're just like Jesus towards your son, and you'll reach out and give him your arms and say, "Thank you, son. It takes a good man to do what you just did. I forgive you." Whatever you can thank God for before you see it, Jesus will let you see it.

Do you believe the Lord is going to heal you "sometime"? Do you believe He's going to deliver your child "sometime"? He's not going to do it, because "sometime" never comes. God is a *now* God, and faith is right now.

A preacher who believed in the great works of God told me one time: "We're praying for my wife's mother, Brother Norvel. The doctors have already told us that there's no hope, and we're praying; but if God doesn't intervene, she's going to die."

"Well, then," I said, "she's going to die."

There was no faith in that man's statement, not even one word of victory. All he had was a bunch of "if's" and "why's" and "if God doesn't do it."

There is no such thing as "if God doesn't do it." If it is a promise to you from the Bible, there is no such thing as "if God doesn't do it." Get that out of your mind, out of your vocabulary.

If that is how you pray, you might as well punch the balloon and walk off. I can tell you right now God isn't going to do the miracle for you. Don't walk around saying, "If God doesn't do it, I guess I will just have to suffer." Put on your "suffering clothes" then, because that is what you are going to get!

If you want God to do anything for you, you've got to show Him that you have faith in Him. Worship Him, ask Him, then thank Him. Show Him now. Don't wait until tomorrow. He wants to manifest Himself to you today. He wants you to accept Him right now on the basis of your faith.

8
Give Him Thanks

8
Give Him Thanks

**Offer unto God thanksgiving; and pay thy vows unto
the Most high: And call upon me in the day of trouble: I
will deliver thee, and thou shalt glorify me.**

Psalm 50:14,15

Some people ask me, "Brother Norvel, why are you
saying I should thank and praise the Lord when I don't
know if I have received from Him what I am praising
Him for? I didn't see anything when I prayed, and I
don't see anything now."

Let's look at the book of Psalms, chapter 50, verses
14 and 15. It says:

**Offer unto God thanksgiving; and pay thy vows unto
the most High:**

**And call upon me in the day of trouble: I will deliver
thee, and thou shalt glorify me.**

I guarantee you this: when you get delivered, you
will glorify the Lord! Right now, you may have a stack
of bills on your desk that can't be paid; but when the
money comes in and you get them all paid, you will
glorify the Lord!

Your leg may be crooked right now; but if you will
worship God and praise Him, one day your healing will
come. It may take time — maybe six months, a year, two

years or three years — but it will come to pass. Remember, faith doesn't have a watch, because faith can't tell time.

You will wake up one morning, and your crooked leg will be just as normal as your other one. And when it is, you will be like that crippled man who was healed at the Gate Beautiful. (Acts 3:8.) You will throw back your cover, jump out of bed and praise God all around the house!

When He delivers you, God said you would glorify His name, and you will too!

Don't Question God

Look at Luke, chapter 17. Follow me closely because you're going to love this.

> And it came to pass, as he went to Jerusalem, that he passed through the midst of Samaria and Galilee.
>
> And as he entered into a certain village, there met him ten men that were lepers, which stood afar off:
>
> And they lifted up their voices, and said, Jesus, Master, have mercy on us.
>
> And when he saw them, he said unto them, Go shew yourselves unto the priests.
>
> **verses 11-14a**

Listen, if you ever ask Jesus to heal you or to give you a miracle and He tells you to go downtown and pass out tracts, don't question Him. Go get some tracts and go downtown as fast as you can and start passing out those tracts. I guarantee you that while you're passing out those tracts or while you're on your way downtown that you'll be healed.

Don't ever question God. I don't understand God, and neither will you. You may want to understand why before you do what He says, but God is not going to tell you anything except what to do. Don't question God. He knows exactly what He is doing. Just obey Him.

Obedience Is Better Than Sacrifice
So these men decided to do what Jesus said to do. They decided to obey Him.

> **And it came to pass, that, as they went, they were cleansed.**
>
> **verse 14b**

Now read closely. Every part of the New Testament that you fail to obey, you will have to sacrifice. In 1 Samuel 15:22 He says it this way: **. . . to obey is better than sacrifice, and to hearken than the fat of rams.**

What would have happened if those ten men had decided not to do what Jesus had said. Besides, they still had leprosy. Why should they go to the priest and be cleansed when they weren't even healed yet? Well, that's what you call acting in faith. They didn't see it yet, but they believed what Jesus had said and acted as if it were so.

And **as they went, they were cleansed** (v. 14). By the time they got to the priest, they were healed, and the priests could pronounce them clean. But they had to obey. If they hadn't obeyed, they would have sacrificed their healing. They would have gone without even though Jesus had already provided it and told them what to do to receive it.

Worship Him With a Thankful Heart
Now notice closely what happens in the next verse.

**And one of them, when he saw that he was healed,
turned back, and with a loud voice glorified God.**

**And fell down on his face at his feet, giving him
thanks: and he was a Samaritan.**

verses 15,16

I hope to God that you think like this man did.
When he saw what Jesus had done, he was grateful. He
was so grateful that he glorified God with a loud voice.
He wasn't embarrassed. He wasn't ashamed. He was
happy. He was glad, and everyone knew it.

Then he fell down on his face at Jesus's feet and gave
thanks. What was he doing? He was worshipping Him.
He was praising Him. He was giving Him thanks.

**And Jesus answering said, Were there not ten
cleansed? but where are the nine?**

**There are not found that returned to give glory to
God, save this stranger.**

**And he said unto him, Arise, go thy way: thy faith
hath made thee whole.**

verses 17-19

This man, because he was thankful, got a double
dose of what Jesus had for him. Not only was he healed,
but he was made whole. You see, when a person got
leprosy in those days, it usually ate away a person's
finger or toe or nose or ear.

But this man, a Samaritan at that, gave glory to God
and was thankful when Jesus healed him. Jesus then
turned around and made him whole. He gave him a
double dose. If his finger had been missing, now it had
grown back. If his toe had been missing, now it had
grown back. God is a miracle-working God, and it isn't
anything for him to put back in place a part that's been

missing. All you have to do is look to Him believing and giving thanks.

I Started Following the Lord

I've been following the Lord for many years since He visited me one night as I was driving down the highway. I had been attending an executive board meeting in Columbus, Ohio, about two hundred miles from home. As I was driving along that night, the Spirit of God came upon me for an hour and a half!

If Jesus ever rides with you in your car for an hour and a half, you will be as wild for Him as I am now! It is like being on a one-way street. You can only go in one direction, and there is no return. When the Lord Jesus Christ comes to visit you like that, you might as well forget about your executive position. You might as well forget about your business and just start following Him.

"What do you mean 'forget about your business'? *You* didn't."

Basically I did. I only had one business at that time, but it was successful. I was living in another world in Indianapolis, Indiana. I was a businessman, an executive, a member of the church, but there was no room for Spirit-filled people and their beliefs about the Holy Spirit and His gifts in my life. Besides, there weren't very many Spirit-filled believers in Indianapolis in those days.

I figured my whole family would be so pleased when they found out how the Lord had come to me as I was driving home that night. But when I told them about it, they didn't go for it, and I wound up with my nine-year-old daughter just given to me to raise!

After that the Lord had me and my daughter move to Cleveland, Tennessee. The Bible says, **...and a little child shall lead them** (Isa. 11:6). My daughter wanted to move to Cleveland, Tennessee, and I would have done anything to help her, so we moved there.

I Obeyed His Leading

It was a stormy, rainy night when I moved, and I had my little nine-year-old girl hanging on to me. We both were brokenhearted. I had a broken heart from the top of my head to the bottom of my feet, and the call of God was all over me.

The Lord God Himself started visiting with me two or three times a week. But I didn't think there was any way that the Spirit of God would ever use a man who was divorced, even though it wasn't my fault I was divorced. I just knew that God would never use me, but I couldn't figure out why He was visiting me so often and so strong.

After moving to Cleveland, Tennessee, I met a Pentecostal preacher and, the day I met him, the Lord said to me, "I want you to talk to him."

So I said, "For some reason, sir, the Lord wants me to talk to you."

When we got to my business office, we sat down to talk. I told him my story in detail. Then I asked him a question.

"What do you think is going to happen to a fellow like me? I am just a businessman. I have the call of God all over me, but I don't really know anything about God. The only thing I know is that He is nice and the devil is mean. What do you think is going to happen to a fellow like me?"

"Well, Norvel, you need to start where you are. Just start doing the little things."

"The little things? What little things?"

"Helping people," he said. "You love young people, so help them."

The pastor I was talking with was working a lot those days in the ministry of helps, reaching out to people.

"Did you ever feed the poor?"

"No," I said. "I've never fed the poor."

"Then start feeding the poor. God finds great favor with people who feed the poor."

"Oh, really?"

"That's right. Start helping people. Help other businessmen find God. Just start working in the ministry of helps any way you can."

"But I have never heard of the ministry of helps before." I really didn't know what that was, but I was willing to learn.

After I began to really follow the Lord, I worked seven years in the ministry of helps. I didn't know then that God had a public ministry for me.

I Got Baptized in the Holy Spirit

Later on, that Pentecostal preacher invited me to come to his church and teach a Sunday school class. So I did. I was planning to leave after the class at that Pentecostal church and go back to my church for Sunday morning service, but the Spirit of God spoke to me as I was going up the steps. He said, "Stay here for this service and show respect." So I stayed.

During the service, a woman who was sitting close to me started speaking in tongues. I had never heard anything like that before, and I thought she was a mental case! But I found out after the service that she was normal.

I thought, "Now that's strange. How can somebody talk like she did in the service and be normal?"

But like a man said, you start fooling around with people who have the baptism of the Holy Spirit, and it is like walking on a slippery creek bank. One of these days you will slip in! Well, eventually I did. I fooled around those Full Gospel people for a while, and it wasn't long until I was baptized in the Holy Spirit and speaking in tongues like the rest of them.

I Worked in the Ministry of Helps

Then I started working with a group from Lee College called "Pioneers For Christ," and I started visiting the Lee College chapel services.

At the time, I owned a restaurant, and it was loaded every day with Lee College students. That was one of my business investments that I had bought a number of years before.

In those days there were no restaurants in that area, so my place became a Lee College hangout, totally packed every Friday and Saturday night. All the college kids who came in there loved me, and they invited me to chapel service. I would go there and get blessed.

The group of Lee College young people that I worked with were a dedicated bunch of kids. They called themselves "Pioneers For Christ," and they *were!*

"What does 'Pioneers For Christ' mean?"

It means they will just go out and pioneer anything! They will make things happen where there is nothing.

When I started working with them, I loved every one of them. In my entire life I had never seen such dedication among young people. And I will never forget them.

They used to work an area that was like a city dump. Once they found a woman with two or three little children who had been sleeping under a tree for several nights because they didn't have a home to go to. The Pioneers For Christ built her a little place around that tree. It was a couple of little rooms made out of slabs that they picked up at the sawmill. You know, "Where there's a will there's a way."

Those Lee College students were a bunch of workers. They had to work their way through school, because they weren't overloaded with money.

Bible school students usually aren't overloaded with money. But it doesn't make any difference. If you are a pioneer for Christ and you find a woman under a tree sleeping with her children, you can build her a house under that tree when you don't have a dime. It all depends on how much pioneer blood you have in you.

After they built that house, I went there one day to pray for that woman. When I walked in to that little place, flies were everywhere. A little girl walked up to me with a dirty, stinking milk bottle in her hand. It looked like she hadn't changed clothes in six months!

"Mister, we don't have no food. Our little baby only has this much milk." She held up that stinking bottle to show me.

When I looked down at her as she looked up at me and said that, the Holy Spirit inside my belly began to rise up and half choke me. I broke down and began to weep. There is so much we have to be thankful for.

Be Thankful Here and I'll Promote You

As I walked out, I saw myself with the tailor-made suit on my back and the Cadillac parked there. I looked up to heaven and said: "Oh, God, is this my ministry? Is this what You are giving me? Is this what I left the church I used to go to for: a city dump ministry? God, is this what You have for me?"

Now some people say that God won't talk to you in an audible voice. But He will sometimes. On the isle of Patmos the apostle John heard a great voice as the sound of a trumpet talking to him. (Rev. 1:10.)

While the apostle Peter was on a housetop praying, he fell into a trance, saw a vision and heard a voice from heaven. (Acts 10:9-16.) God was getting Peter ready and preparing him to take the Gospel to the Gentiles.

When I cried out to God that day, I heard a voice come down from heaven to me. He said: "Son, be thankful to Me here, and I'll promote you. I only promote people I can trust."

Now you can understand the ministry of helps and the depth of it. I didn't know that God Himself had created the ministry of helps in the doctrines of the church. There is much about the doctrines of the church that most people don't know anything about. My friend, when God says something and He puts a doctrine in the church, no man has a right to take it away.

So one of the doctrines of the New Testament church is the ministry of helps. (1 Cor. 12:28.) Every church in the world that doesn't have a ministry of helps — to train young people, to feed the poor, to help all people in need — is out of God's will.

"How do you know?" you may say.

Well, I can read. All you have to do to find out if you are out of God's will is to read the Bible for yourself. God has set some gifts and doctrines in the church. If you don't have what He put in the church, how can you be in God's perfect will? There is no way you can if you are not going to believe what He said and receive the things that He has put in the church and add those things to your life.

For example, it would please God if all nine of the gifts of the Spirit talked about in 1 Corinthians 12 were operating in your church as the Spirit wills. The sad part of it is that many churches in the world don't even believe in them. Some pastors get behind the pulpit and make light of them. Some actually make fun of them.

Some make fun of tongues and interpretation. I wouldn't have that much nerve!

I found out from God a long time ago that anybody who makes fun of Jesus and the Gospel and the Holy Ghost will not live his life out. You can't make fun of anything about God, Jesus, the Bible, the Holy Ghost, and the church or any of its doctrines. You can't make fun of them and expect to live happily ever after.

Make up your mind that when God sets doctrines in the church, that's the way it is. No man has a right to change it. "If you want to get along with Me," God is saying in the Bible, "you had better read the Bible and follow it. Any man — I don't care who he is or what he looks like — that adds to it or takes away from it, the plagues of the world will go to him."

If you will start spending time with people who are dedicated to God and go to prayer meetings with them, you will learn how to pray. God will give you the desires of your heart if you will just seek God from your heart, with true motives.

Worship and praise God first. Then pray that He will show you where He wants to use you. Be thankful for wherever He places you, and eventually He will promote you!

Be Thankful For the
Ministry He Gives You

Some people live in the world of wondering. They say, "I wonder what my ministry is." People say to me: "Brother Norvel, can you tell me what my ministry is?" or "Brother Norvel, can we pray and see where I should go and what I should do? I need to know what my ministry is. Can you tell me?"

I say, "Oh, yes, I can tell you what your ministry is."

It is knocking on doors and passing out tracts, feeding the poor, and helping the needy.

"But I don't want to do that kind of thing, Brother Norvel. I'm not talking about that. I'm talking about my ministry."

"That *is* your ministry," I tell them. I was satisfied with that kind of ministry for seven years. I didn't want a public ministry. I didn't ask for a public ministry. That wasn't what I was looking for. If you are looking for a public ministry and nothing else, *He's* not calling you. That's you.

Instead of refusing to do anything but a public ministry, be willing to do *whatever* God wants you to do, *when* He wants you to do it, *where* He wants you to do it, and *how* He wants you to do it. Just be willing.

Someone may ask, "Brother Norvel, what if God told you to go back full time into the ministry of helps and let somebody else do all that preaching?"

If God told me that, I would say, "Praise the Lord!"

"Would you go back to Lee College and start working with the Pioneers For Christ again?"

I would go, and I would go quickly! And I'm not kidding.

Don't get hung up on being a great speaker. I do a lot of preaching, but I don't get hung up on it. I receive thousands of invitations. Not only that, people are offering me plenty of money just to come and speak for one night. Only one night!

These days I go to meetings all over the country, from the East Coast to the West Coast and even to foreign countries. I was in South Africa once, and I couldn't believe it myself. Five thousand people came to the meeting, and I had never been to South Africa before in my life.

I asked them, "Before I walked up behind the pulpit today, how many people in here knew me?"

There were probably about three thousand hands that went up. I couldn't believe it!

"How did you know me?" I asked. "I've never been here before."

They just kind of laughed and said, "We know you, Brother Norvel."

After that, I went to speak at another convention. There was a whole group of people there from Nigeria, and I had never been to Nigeria in my life. But that whole clan of Nigerian people brought me gifts.

"Why are you bringing me gifts?" I asked. "How do you know me?"

"We know you, Brother Norvel. We love you, Brother Norvel. We want you to come to Nigeria, Brother Norvel. Won't you please come to Nigeria?"

"Well," I said, "you keep that up very long, and I guess I will have to go to Nigeria!"

As I said, I didn't ask God for a public ministry. I wasn't looking for one. But because I worshipped and praised God, He promoted me. And He will do the same for you. He wants to pour His abundant blessings down from heaven onto you. Worship Him for Who He is; praise Him for what He has done.

Prayer of Salvation

If you haven't accepted the Lord Jesus Christ as your personal Savior, pray this prayer below and accept Him. Enter into a covenant with Him, begin to worship and praise Him and come on in to the abundant life that will set you free. If He will do it for me, He will do it for you too.

Dear Heavenly Father,

Forgive me for anything I have done or said that would be against Your will. Wash me clean. Let me be white as snow. Let me have a tender, sweet relationship with You. I want to know You more. Please come and be my Lord and my Savior.

Let Your power melt all the world out of me, so that I can be steadfast like the Rock, Christ Jesus. I love You and worship You. Thank You for sending Your Son, Jesus, to me and to the world. In Jesus' name, amen.

For a complete list of tapes and
books by Norvel Hayes, write:

Norvel Hayes
P. O. Box 1379
Cleveland, TN 37311

Please feel free to include your prayer requests and comments when you write.

Prayer To Receive the
Baptism in the Holy Spirit

According to the New Testament, Jesus wants to baptize everybody on earth with the Holy Spirit, and He wants everybody on earth to speak in other tongues. So you can base what you believe on the Scriptures, I have listed a few key passages for you to refer to. See John 14:16,17; Acts 2:1-4;16-18,32,33,38,39; Acts 8:12,14-17; Acts 9:17; Acts 19:1-3,6; Acts 10:44-46; 1 Cor. 14:2,18; John 7:37-39; Luke 11:11-13; Luke 24:49; Acts 1:8.

The only responsibility of the Holy Spirit to you or anybody else is to give you the utterance like He did on the day of Pentecost, but you do the speaking. As you read this prayer, receive the baptism of the Holy Spirit by faith and begin to speak out in faith any sounds or syllables that rise up within you.

Dear Heavenly Father,

I come before You now with an open heart to receive all You have for me. I have already accepted the Lord Jesus as the Lord and Savior of my life, so now I open myself to receive the power of Your Holy Spirit.

You said in Your Word that if I asked, I would receive, so I ask You now to fill me to overflowing with Your precious Holy Spirit.

I receive Him now by faith and expect to speak with other tongues as He gives me the utterance. In Jesus' name, amen.

Norvel Hayes is a successful businessman, internationally renowned bible teacher, and founder of several Christian ministries in the U.S. and abroad.

Brother Hayes founded *New Life Bible College,* located in Cleveland, Tennessee, in 1977. *New Life Bible Church* grew out of the Bible schools' chapel services. The Bible School offers a two-year diploma and off-campus correspondence courses. Among it's many other out-reaches, the church ministers God's Word and hot meal daily to the poor through the *New Life Soup Kitchen.*

Brother Hayes is also the founder and president of *New Life Maternity Home,* a ministry dedicated to the spiritual, physical and financial need of young girls during pregnancy; *Campus Challenge,* an evangelistic outreach that distributes Christian literature on College campuses across America; *Street Reach,* a ministry dedicated to runaway teens located in Daytona Beach, Florida; and *Children's Home,* an orphanage home and education center located in India.

Known internationally for his dynamic exposition of the Word of God, Brother Hayes spends most of his time teaching and ministering God's deliverance and healing power in churches, college classrooms, conventions and seminars, around the world.

Other Books by Norvel Hayes

Worship	*The Blessing of Obedience*
Don't Let the Devil Steal Your Destiny	*Let Not Your Heart Be Troubled*
Why You Should Speak in Tongues	*The Number One Way To Fight the Devil*
What To Do for Healing	*Confession Brings Possession*
Misguided Faith	*How To Live and Not Die*
	How To Get Your Prayers Answered